THE SOUTHERN WAY

Issue No 3

CONTENTS

© Kevin Robertson (Noodle Books) and the various contributors 2008

ISBN 978-1-906419-03-5

First published in 2008 by Kevin Robertson
under the **NOODLE BOOKS** imprint
PO Box 279
Corhampton
SOUTHAMPTON
SO32 3ZX
www.kevinrobertsonbooks.co.uk

Printed in England by
Ian Allan Printing Ltd
Hersham, Surrey

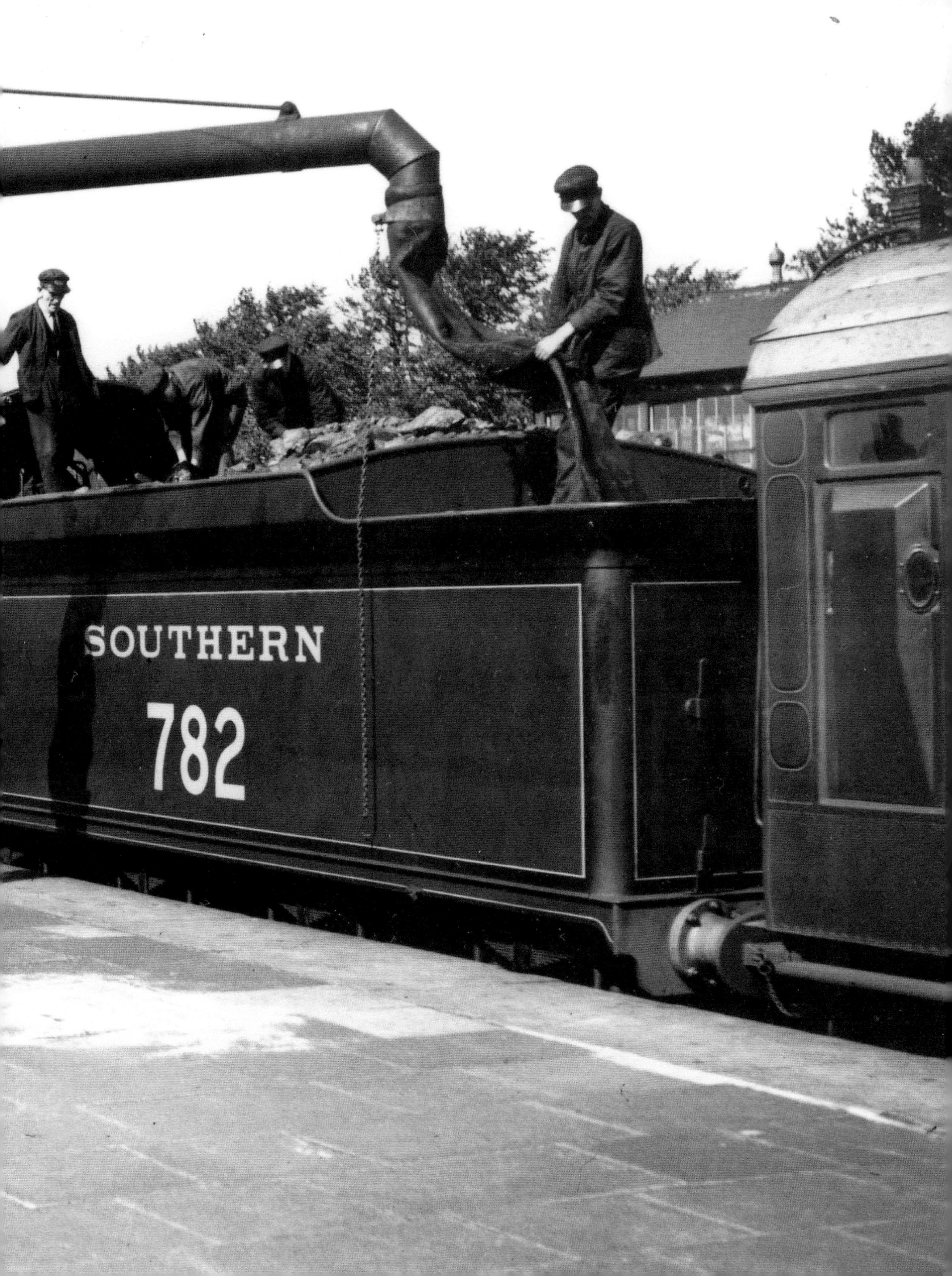
SOUTHERN
782

Editorial Introduction

I have to confess to yet again attempting to pour the proverbial quart into a pint pot. Before the start of every issue I set out a schedule of what I would like to include. Personal preference, of course, comes into the equation but so I hope does what, I trust, will be of interest.

The problem comes that despite this being the second of three issues for 2008, not including the separate Colour Special, it is still very difficult to try to be topical and attempt to follow any theme or indeed the launch of a new model. I say this as from a marketing perspective obviously, if there is a new product in the shops, then it follows that an issue of 'SW' with a similar feature could well be of mutual interest.

Sometimes it works and the two do tie in. Mostly though it does not and I shall not attempt to manipulate an issue just for that reason. Neither, you will be pleased to hear, shall I plan for an eventual monthly issue. I want both of us, you and I to enjoy what we have, not see it as a chore nor a drain on resources.

As before in these introductions, I can still only be humbled by the response. Sadly I have not pleased everyone. I have to report receiving an extremely vitriolic e-mail from an anonymous individual, similarly despatched from a location that would not accept return correspondence. If said person reads this then all I can say, if you had been planning a similar idea as 'SW' yourself, get in touch and let us talk. I have said before and will say it again, let us pool ideas for the benefit of all - especially whilst the material and knowledge is accessible.

For the future all I can say is I am starting to be wary about even setting out definite plans for the next issue, so much worthwhile material continues to appear. As the advertisers say, 'Watch this space', it may be slightly portentous, but I don't think you will be disappointed.

Kevin Robertson

Left - Out of the mist at Eastleigh. Amongst the collection of material loaned to us by Howard Butler was this startling view of the new 21C1 at Eastleigh, no doubt taken when brand new in 1941. The photograph has not been enhanced or manipulated in any way. The effect, whether intended or co-incidental, is certainly profound and no doubt had the same impression on others. One interesting comment from the period is that certain of the work-force objected to the notion of an express passenger engine at a time when Britain was literally fighting for survival. The common notion has always been that the type were designated 'mixed-traffic' in order to secure approval from Government for their construction. Possibly then the sanction of the workforce was similarly required. (We have further views of 21C1 from this period to accompany a future article.)

Howard Butler collection

Previous page - Salisbury, Platform 4 on a unreported date. 'King Arthur' class 4-6-0 No 782 'Sir Brian' is being prepared ready for its onward run to the west and with the able assistance of two additional men, under the watchful gaze of a seemingly surly driver. Could the bowler hat clad individual be a Locomotive Inspector?

Taunton Model Railway Group

Front cover - A chance conversation and the opportunity to record what is a rare scene, a somewhat grimy 'S11' No 30403 at Bournemouth with mixed Southern and British Railways identification. At the time this was one of two survivors of the class, the other was No 30398, working from Bournemouth, where the view was taken. Despite having a smokebox numberplate, the engine was never repainted in its allotted lined black livery and was withdrawn in September 1951. Therefore a colour view such as this is unusual indeed.

Pursey Short, courtesy Chris Woods / Colour Rail

Rear cover - Remaining in the Bournemouth / Dorset area, is this rural record of the Swanage branch near Furzebrook. Colour views from the 1950s are rare enough, especially one without a train. Dare we say that an article by Mark Abbott on Furzebrook is also pending for a future issue.

Paul Hersey collection

Left - This early lithograph is looking south from Chapel Hill, Basingstoke, towards the town, close to the derelict Holy Ghost Chapel, with the railway crossing from left to right. The GWR station is prominent on the left with the LSWR facilities behind. Hants County Library.

Centre - A view of the station approaches just prior to the demolition of the main station building to make way for the quadrupling. There was little choice by the LSWR, as the up platform buildings formed the boundary with the established GWR station. The single storey building on the right is of interest. It is just possible this may be at least part of the short-lived station accommodation appearing on the early ground plan, that was superseded by the familiar two-storey building circa 1849. Railway Magazine. *Lower* - The station building awaits it's fate as seen here around 1900. The splendid telegraph pole to the right was a notable feature of the station for many years.

BASINGSTOKE

Part 1 - The years down to 1904

Roger Simmonds

From its earliest years, Basingstoke has been considered by the travelling public as the gateway to the South and West of England. On the opening of the London & Southampton Railway throughout, on 11th May 1840, the town was the first significant stopping place from the then London terminus at Nine Elms.

The settlement at Basing formed an important centre in Saxon times, and later was the scene of a notable defence by the Marquis of Winchester against Cromwell's army. The early markets held here were mentioned in Domesday and the annual fairs played an important part in the life of the town and surrounding farming community. King James I once described the place as 'villa antiqua et populosa' (an ancient and popular town).

The first mode of transport (other than the established cart roads) to reach the town was the Basingstoke Canal, first proposed in 1769. During the following year, a meeting of the townspeople in the town hall resolved 'that the making of a navigable canal from Basingstoke to communicate with the River Thames at a place called Monkey Island, near Windsor, will be of great public utility'. Opened in 1796, the canal was only moderately successful, and the emergence of the rival Kennett and Avon in 1810 saw its commercial viability in the balance. The planned extension to Salisbury and the West never materialised, and it remained very much a local affair.

Around 1800, the town was still largely agriculturally dependent, serving for the most part a very limited and thinly populated hinterland; its main function was the provision of markets for the local farmers. As such, it provided the traditional crafts and trades associated with such an economy. By 1837, it was noted that the town was 'gradually increasing in size and importance'; the population had increased from 2,589 in 1801 to 3,600 by the middle 1830s. The imminent establishment of the railway in Basingstoke initiated its slow change from a thriving market town to a manufacturing centre, with a consequent housing expansion.

The first signs of impending railway development in the area occurred at Shapley Heath (Winchfield) on 6th October 1834, where the London & Southampton engineer, Francis Giles, had engaged the contractors Messrs. Treadwell for the section between Wey and Basing. Giles's policy had been to employ a number of small contractors working concurrently at various locations on the line; the L & S Minute Book recorded some of them, including Messrs. Bernard Richardson, David Mackintosh and Thomas Green (for construction of bridges). Progress was slow and Giles, heavily criticised for his methods of working, was eventually replaced by Joseph Locke, in January 1837.

Matters now took a fresh impetus with a new contractor, Thomas Brassey, appointed to take over a considerable part of the unfinished works from the London end to Winchester. Work from this time went forward at a greatly increased pace, with Brassey gaining much recognition and justifiable prestige for his efforts in securing the completion of a previously poorly co-ordinated and haphazard set of works along the route of the main line.

As far as Basingstoke was concerned, the early difficulties with Giles had confined progress out to the parish of Elvetham (beyond Hook village) where excavations had been made as early as the winter of 1834. It would appear that by 1837 the station area had been marked out by Treadwell, and by the following year it was almost ready to receive the first metals. The contract for the difficult section from Basingstoke to Winchester was awarded to Brassey in May 1838; the route was different to that laid down in the L&S Act (being amended in the 1837 Sessions), but still involved heavy earthworks in order to cross the Popham Beacons - this involved the removal of some 1,400,000 cubic yards of material.

On 24th September 1838, the L&S finally entered the County of Hampshire when the section from Woking to Shapley Heath (Winchfield) was opened for public use. Work continued on the section to Basingstoke, but not without some difficulties. The embankment between Hook and Basing was found to be unstable, and persisted in slipping outwards; this was only checked after extensive pile driving.

On 17th May 1839, the much-encouraged L&S Directors resolved 'that the Traffic and General Purposes Committee be empowered to make such arrangements as they think proper with respect to the opening of the line between Winchfield and Basingstoke'. The latter town was consequently 'en fete' on 10th June, when that section of the line was opened.

A view taken after the improvements of 1874. These included raising the up and down platform height to 2'6" and extending both some 285 feet over Chapel Street Bridge. This necessitated the widening of the Bridge which fortuitously by chance anticipated the quadrupling thirty years later. A new refreshment room was erected at the west end of the down platform, with the original dining room at the London end converted to WC's. Also at this time on the up platform the refreshment room and urinals located at the east end were demolished and relocated at the west or country end. Shunting horses were a common sight at this time in and around both the LSWR & GWR stations. The LSWR stables were approved on 15th June 1859 (stables for the latter were located in the GW goods yard). It was reported by the LSWR Traffic Committee on 5th January 1903 that unfortunately a shunting horse had been killed, presumably having been hit by a moving train.   *Lens of Sutton Association*

The *Hampshire Chronicle* reported:

LONDON AND SOUTHAMPTON RAILWAY.
'*On Monday the line of road from the Winchfield and Hartley Row station was opened to the public as far as Basingstoke, a distant of eight miles; and on the same day from Southampton to Winchester, leaving only 18 miles to complete the undertaking. A party of the directors and their friends left the terminus at Nine Elms, Vauxhall, at half-past eleven, and arrived at the Winchfield station at about five minutes to one, where a crowd of spectators was assembled, and greeted them with hearty cheers. After a short delay the train proceeded over the new ground to Basingstoke, while upon every height, and at every place where a view could be obtained, groups of anxious and admiring spectators were stationed to watch and applaud the progress of the engine and its bulky train upon its maiden excursion. At about half-past two o'clock the train started from Basingstoke on its return to Winchfield, accomplishing the distance without the slightest accident or annoyance to mar the pleasures of the day. A cold collation was provided at a cottage in* the vicinity of the station, to which about 60 ladies and gentlemen sat down: including Mr. Easthope, M.P. the Chairman of the Company: Mr. T Duncombe, M.P., Mr. Bainbridge, &c. At seven o'clock the party broke up, and the train finally reached Vauxhall at ten minutes past eight.'

Basingstoke's function as a temporary terminus for trains from Nine Elms lasted for just under a year, until the final gap in the main line was filled by the opening of the section to Winchester on 11th May 1840. During this intervening period, passengers had been conveyed by coach between the two stations, the L & S Board stating in 1839 that 'Arrangements have been made to complete the journey to London in five hours and the Directors have provided commodious vehicles for conveying passengers from the Winchester Station to Basingstoke in time to join the railway trains there'.

At this stage in its life Basingstoke station was a compact wayside affair and similar in appearance to those provided at Farnborough, Winchfield, Andover Road (Micheldever) and Winchester. The main station building was a favoured design by William Tite, with size variations to suit the locality. The original drawings

An early view looking south believed to date from shortly after 1865. It was reported on 5th January 1865 that the canopy columns were to be removed following the death of a goods guard. No details of the incident are recorded. Note the low level platforms of the period, these were raised and extended in 1874 as part of a range of improvements to the facilities.

1847, as recorded at the time of the arrival of the Berks and Hants route from Reading. Shown is the east elevation of the down side building. This is the oldest located plan showing an aspect of the station.. The B & H station was located to the right, north of the LSWR as seen in the illustration on page 14.

for Basingstoke appear not to have survived the passage of time, but fortunately an end elevation and ground plan of 1848, showing the east end of the station, did manage to escape the fate of it's contemporaries. This clearly shows a station building of much smaller dimensions than (and to the east of) the known structure swept away in the improvements of 1904. This exciting discovery, apparently unrecorded elsewhere, prompted further research which indicates that the new building (some 80 feet west of the original) was almost certainly erected in 1849 or 1850 - before the opening of the line to Andover. An official 1855 survey clearly shows the

much larger replacement building, obviously reflecting the anticipated increase in passenger traffic which would hopefully result from the extension to the West of England. An 1851 land survey was subsequently uncovered in the local Record Office, which indicated similar dimensions, thus enabling the date of the new structure to be more accurately determined.

A legacy of the L&S proposed Basing and Bath Railway (included in a prospectus of January 1832) was that, despite that line losing out to the rival GWR (whose Bill received the Royal Assent in 1835), the station was laid out with a westerly prospect. This caused the Southampton line to take a south-westerly course beyond the station over a more northerly route than would have otherwise been necessary.

The original facilities were not destined to remain in isolation for long, and in September 1845, following proposals and counter proposals by the LSWR and GWR for westward extensions, the nominally-independent Berks & Hants Railway obtained an Act for lines from Reading to Hungerford and to Basingstoke. This contained an 'equal rates' clause to offer the chastened LSWR a crumb of comfort. However, the LSWR did slightly better in the 1846 Sessions when the Basingstoke and Salisbury Bill succeeded, thus opening up the way for a line to the West.

THE GWR ARRIVES

Progress with the construction of the Basingstoke branch of the Berks & Hants line (now firmly a corporate part of the GWR) was brisk, with the whole works let to Messrs. Rowland Brotherhood. Despite good progress initially, delays were experienced as the new line approached Basingstoke. In previously published material, this has been attributed solely to protracted negotiations with the hostile LSWR. Although this, no doubt, was the major factor, it does also seem likely that the unearthing of numerous ancient graves and artifacts dating from the bronze age (in the approach cutting to the station close to the Reading Road bridge)

Left - The arrival of General Sir Redvers Buller at Basingstoke on his return from the Boar War in November 1900. This view shows the station masters accommodation to the left of the view. Not all was well with the house as in 1883 it was reported that serious drainage and sanitation problems existed and that the house was in an "unhealthy" condition. It must have been in a parlous state as consideration was being given to providing a new house on land adjoining the station. By February 1884, however, sanitary works and other improvements were undertaken, at a cost of £174. 18s.

Lower - Plans to upgrade and transform the station were already in hand when this well known photograph was taken around 1900, just before the reconstruction commenced. The accommodation at this time consisted of (left to right) the 1874 refreshment room with dining room and kitchen behind, a large urinal, ladies waiting room, 3rd, 1st and 2nd class waiting rooms respectively, the booking hall, a small general waiting room, telegraph office and station master's office. The incumbent at this time was probably Mr. J. Gabriel, who arrived in 1896 (replaced by the short-lived Mr. Barnes in January 1902). The staff complement shown in this view expanded somewhat, with the completion of the new station, to 130 men including shunters and signalmen.

Right - Quite an assortment of buildings required to be purchased by the LSWR to enable the new works to proceed, including the public house, the wooden shed seen here and a considerable number of cottages, some of which are seen in the left background. No doubt some of the pub regulars took to imbibing in the close by Rising Sun Inn in Chapel Hill.

Lower - Unlike today, the station was located some distance from the centre of the town and the absence of the urban spread is quite noticeable in this picture. To the right of the LSW station building is what appears to be the old goods transfer shed with the GWR. This may date the photograph to before 1891 when the GW proposed to remove it and handle the work in their newly opened goods shed. In the right foreground are the works of Wallis & Haslam (later Wallis & Stevens) manufacturers of traction engines and road rollers. The firm started in 1860 and together with nearby Thorneycroft's put Basingstoke on the map for these types of vehicles.

stopped work for some time.

The 13½ mile broad gauge line from Southcote Junction finally opened on 1st November 1848. The Board of Trade inspection had taken place on 16th October. The Inspector, Capt. Simmons, found little adverse to report on save a minor indiscretion in the Parliamentary limits of deviation authorised and some loose fastenings in the permanent way. Tantalisingly, 'as with most of the Board's early inspections, virtually nothing is mentioned of the stations or operating arrangements so amply and exhaustively noted in later reports.

Basingstoke townsfolk now had a choice of routes to the Capital, with good services and only a small difference in mileage between the two lines (47m 63ch to Waterloo, and 51m 40ch to Paddington).

The GWR station at the end of the double line from Reading was constructed in timber, with an overall roof contemporaneous in design to other stations of the late 1840s and early 1850s. It was located alongside the LSWR station, on the north side of the Up platform. The obvious differences in the gauges meant that no physical connection between the two systems was possible, and a wooden goods transfer shed was erected between the LSWR Up and GWR Down running lines to facilitate the transfer of merchandise between the companies.

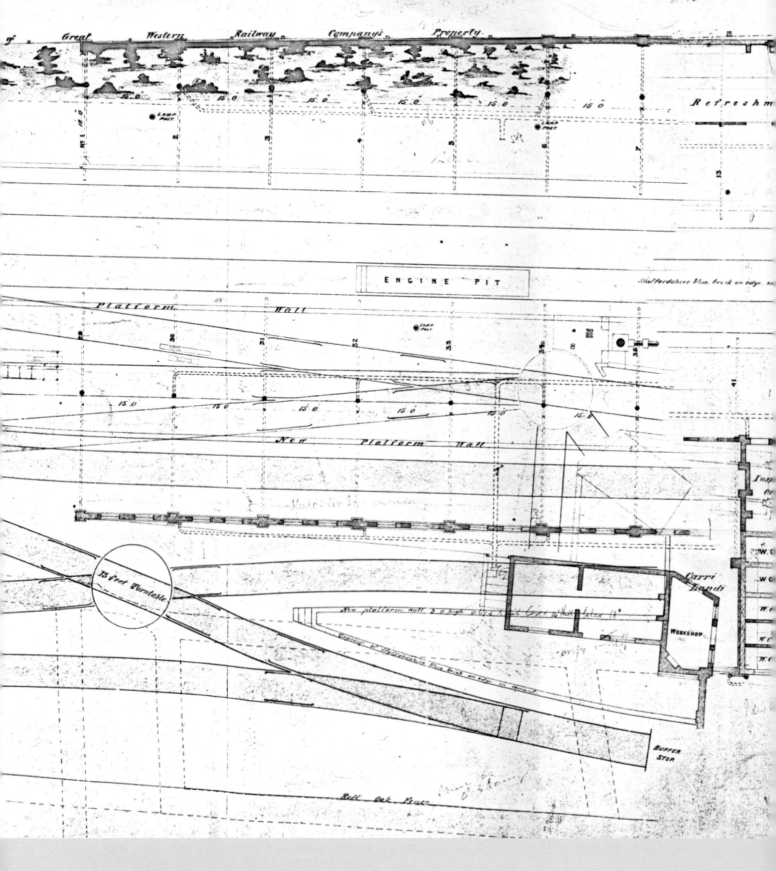

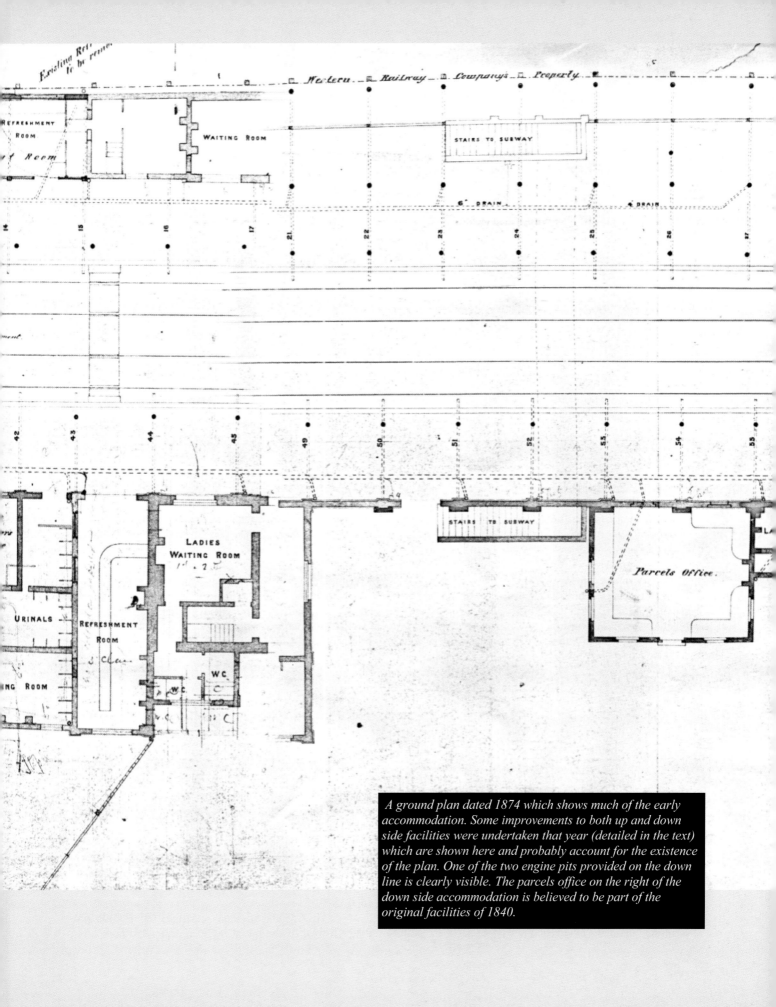

Existing Rev. to be removed.

Western — Railway — Company's — Property

REFRESHMENT ROOM

t Room

WAITING ROOM

STAIRS TO SUBWAY

6" DRAIN   4" DRAIN

14   15   16   17   21   22   23   24   25   26   27

ment.

42   43   44   45   49   50   51   52   53   54   55

LADIES WAITING ROOM

STAIRS TO SUBWAY

Parcels Office.

URINALS

REFRESHMENT ROOM

ING ROOM

W.C.

W.C.

A ground plan dated 1874 which shows much of the early accommodation. Some improvements to both up and down side facilities were undertaken that year (detailed in the text) which are shown here and probably account for the existence of the plan. One of the two engine pits provided on the down line is clearly visible. The parcels office on the right of the down side accommodation is believed to be part of the original facilities of 1840.

Looking west from the London end shows the proximity of the two companies stations. Although there was considerable exchange of traffic between the companies friction arose from time to time. GWR porters went onto the LSWR station to deal with Great Western destined parcels and squabbles broke out on occasions, with accusations that LSWR goods were being inappropriately handled by GW men!. Lens of Sutton Association

Road access to this building was provided from Bunnion Place.

The potential of this north to south connection via Oxford and Reading was soon realised, and external pressure on the GWR to provide the means for standard gauge running came to fruition on 22nd December 1856, when 'narrow' gauge trains were able to work through between Basingstoke and the North via Oxford. The Great Western eventually found little merit in operating both gauges on the line from Reading, and in due course the broad gauge element fell out of use. The seven foot gauge was eventually removed between Southcote Junction and Basingstoke in 1869.

The LSWR had to learn to live with its new neighbour and certainly in the early days there appears to have been very little co-operation. Some indication of this emerges from the Minute Books. As early as 3rd November 1848, a Mr. Markin wrote to the LSWR requesting that a siding be provided for him; the swift reply referred him to the GW Company 'as they may have some inclination to provide such a facility'.

Another example occurred in December 1857, when a letter was received by the LSWR from a Mr. Challis suggesting that a gas lamp be erected to illuminate the arch leading to the Great Western Company's station. Although this would be within the South Western Company's boundary, they advised Mr. Challis that he should write to the GWR.

SOME MINOR IMPROVEMENTS

With the increase in passenger traffic resulting from the interchange between the companies, the LSWR undertook some general improvement work at their station. The Directors approved the provision of a small refreshment room on 22nd December 1848, referring it to the Way & Works Committee 'as to the best mode and cost of providing the facility'. It is believed the new station building was also constructed at the time this work was in hand. An increase in the Gentlemen's toilet facilities was approved in May 1862, following a recommendation from the Station Master, Mr. Gardiner. An interesting and novel suggestion also made by Gardiner at the time was that the signals at the station should be lit with gas; this was recorded in June as to be carried out, but no further reference has been found. Provision for luggage transfer 'between the Up and Down platforms' (presumably a board crossing) was sanctioned on 25th June 1863.

FURTHER EXPANSION

By the end of 1847, construction of the Basingstoke and Salisbury Railway was under way, the contract for the work going to Thomas Brassey. The tender is recorded in the Minute Books as £380,000. The Basingstoke to Andover section was to be given first priority. Initial progress was good, but the effects of the prevailing general economic depression began to bite during 1848, with rising costs and higher land purchase prices than expected. The LSWR was therefore constrained to limit monthly expenditure, and to apply for a two-year extension of powers. This was authorised in June 1849.

By 1851 work had restarted, the LSWR no doubt fearful of the threat by an independent company (formed by a consortium of local landowners) to complete the unfinished works. The line was now to be single, and an amended tender for £74,000 was given to Brassey to complete the line to Andover. Civil engineering work was fairly light through the open chalk countryside on this section and by June 1854 the line was complete.

The Board of Trade inspection took place on 21st June. Capt. Tyler reported that the works had been carried out for a double line, but laid with a single line of rails. He was critical of the fact that the recently-constructed chalk embankments had not been allowed sufficient time to settle, and recommended that the slopes be improved and that 'the speed of trains be restricted to not exceeding 20 miles per hour until the embankments are con-solidated'.

The somewhat haphazard operating methods of railway companies of the day are amplified by the Inspector's comments with reference to Worting Junction: 'The levers for working the points and signals shall be so arranged that they may all be on one side of the line in order that the signalman may not be compelled to cross the line as he would be at present when it becomes necessary for him to work two of the levers'. The South Western reacted smartly, and confirmed to the BOT, in a letter of 23rd June, that the offending levers had been moved from the Down to the Up side of the line. Thus, with the undertaking to restrict the speed of trains, the LSWR were given permission to open the line to the public, which they did on 3rd July. The line was eventually extended to Salisbury (Milford) on 1st May 1857.

Some four years later, the line was doubled between Worting Junction and Andover; this was brought into use with little ceremony following Col. Yolland's inspection for the BOT on 20th December 1861.

AN UNFORTUNATE EVENT

At around this time, Basingstoke was the scene of a mishap concerning one of the formative Salisbury service trains. The *Hampshire Chronicle* recorded on 25th December 1858:

'A serious accident occurred at this station on Wednesday last in consequence of the train, which leaves Southampton at 11.30 am. running into the Salisbury train due at the same place a few minutes previously. The latter train had arrived at its proper time, and was in the act of shunting into a siding when the Southampton train approached, and although the danger signals were all properly exhibited, the driver, from some unexplained cause, was unable to bring up his engine in sufficient time to avoid a collision, by which the two last carriages of the Salisbury train were

knocked off the rails, one of them falling completely over on the down line, and seriously hurting several of its occupants. The accident was observed by Mr. Williams, the Station Master, who, powerless to prevent the collision, after it had occurred, instantly summoned his forces to extricate the alarmed passengers, and in a very short time all were got out and comfortably attended in the station and adjoining hotel. Two of the occupants of a second-class carriage were so severely shaken that it was deemed desirable for them to remain at Basingstoke; but all the other passengers went on to London in less than an hour. ...'

THE SECOND STATION REDEVELOPMENT

During the years following the provision of improved facilities (c.1849), the town enjoyed increasing prosperity, and some twenty years later had reached the point where the station's resources were again proving inadequate, and outwardly were more akin to a wayside country affair. Train services were expanding and the company's engines were becoming more powerful, permitting longer train lengths on the principal services. These and other factors, necessitated improvements at many of the major stations on the system.

The LSWR therefore undertook a series of upgrading works at Basingstoke in 1874 to meet the contemporary requirements. On the Down side, the small refreshment room of 1848 (located at the London end) was replaced by a new, enlarged facility at the west end of the main station building. This was on the ground floor and included a separate dining room and kitchen. The original refreshment room was converted to WC accommodation. A new Inspectors office was provided at the extreme west end of the building, over the site of the former buffer stops of the Down 'bay'.

On the Up side, the early refreshment room and urinals at the London end were demolished. These were replaced at the country end by improved structures. Both platforms were raised to a height of 2ft 6in and extended by about 285ft in a westerly direction over Chapel Street bridge. The bridge was widened to give an equivalent four-road width, and the back road (later known as number 6) leading from the GW station was put in by extending the Up siding. Chapel Street bridge thus consisted of two 28ft-wide trestles side by side, with a 4ft-wide footbridge for pedestrians on the north side of the structure. A ground plan of the full facilities existing in 1884 can be seen on pages 12/13.

An interesting proposal of 1871 might have seen the establishment of the LSWR Carriage and Wagon Works to the west of the station, near Worting. The company extolled the virtues of building the works here to the town's officials, 'so manifestly advantageous

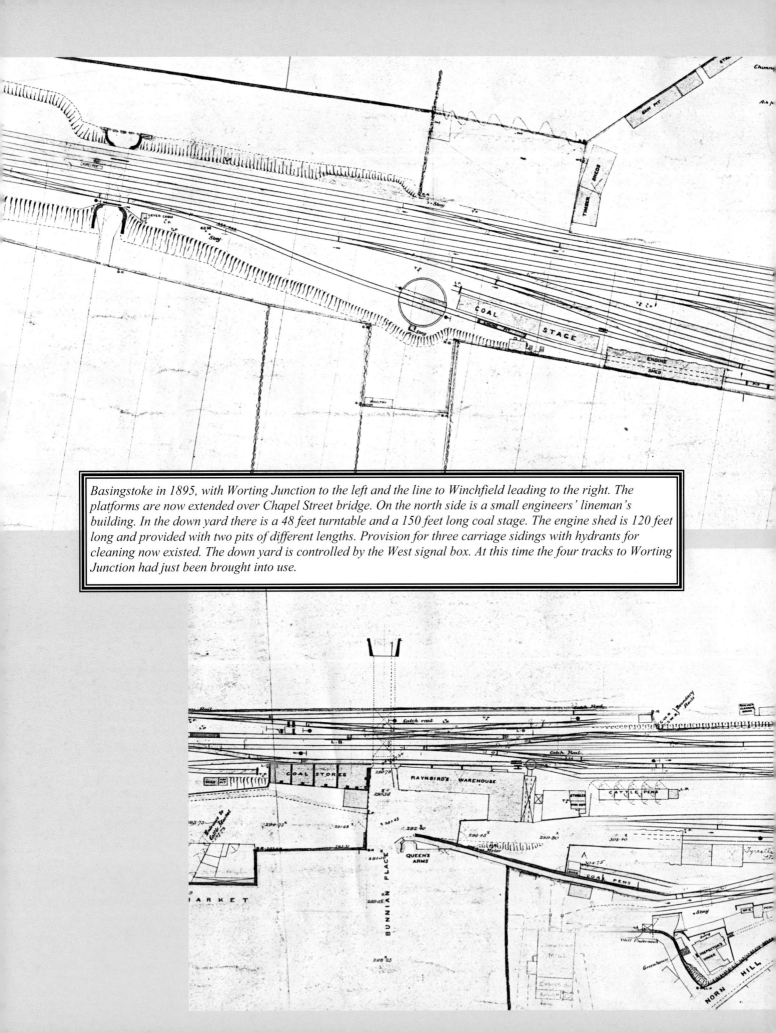

Basingstoke in 1895, with Worting Junction to the left and the line to Winchfield leading to the right. The platforms are now extended over Chapel Street bridge. On the north side is a small engineers' lineman's building. In the down yard there is a 48 feet turntable and a 150 feet long coal stage. The engine shed is 120 feet long and provided with two pits of different lengths. Provision for three carriage sidings with hydrants for cleaning now existed. The down yard is controlled by the West signal box. At this time the four tracks to Worting Junction had just been brought into use.

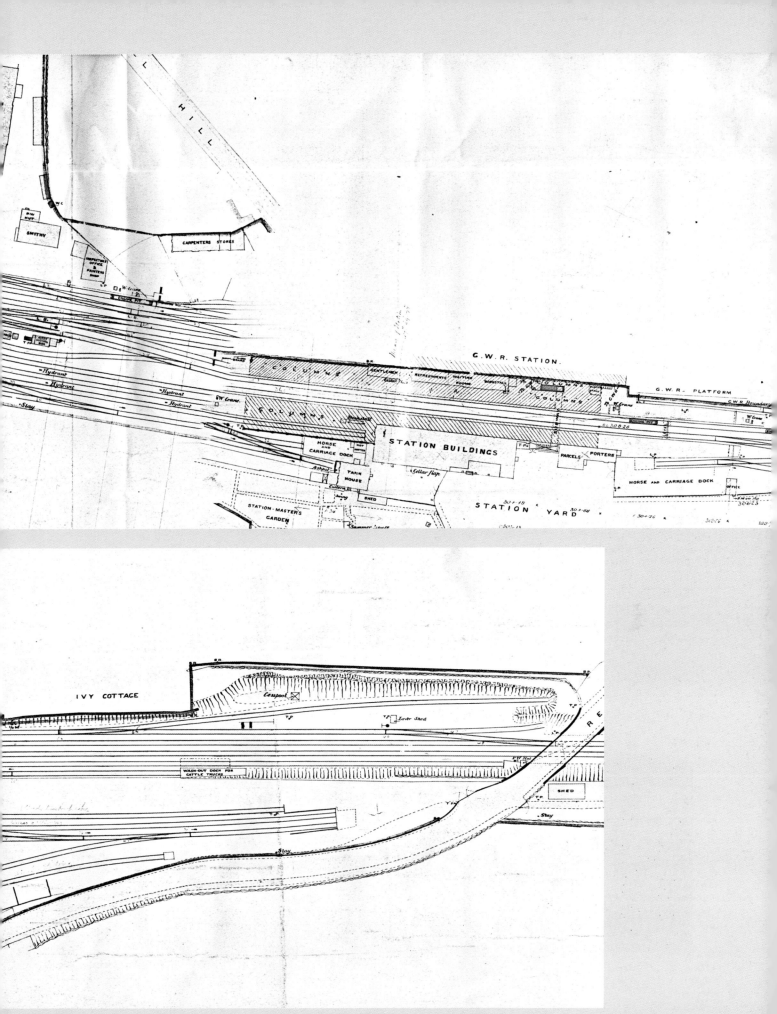

to the town'. However, Basingstoke Corporation saw things differently and took a conservative view, strongly opposing the plan, resolving 'that the works would bring a class of people to the town that would lower its reputation'. By 1879, the apparent threat had disappeared, the LSWR approving the construction of the Works at Bishopstoke (Eastleigh).

Other improvements were carried out in the station area during December 1878, when the LSWR/ GWR connection was modified by the provision of a new crossover connecting the South-Western Up main with the Great Western line. This modification was long overdue and avoided the necessity of trains from Reading having to shunt back onto the LSWR Down line to reach the Up main. The work was paid for by the GWR, at an estimated cost of £70.

In July 1882, the LSWR found it necessary to completely relay the junction at Worting, although this action may not have been entirely successful. It was subsequently reported to the Directors (on 11th June 1884) that several passengers had complained to the Board of Trade that Salisbury-bound trains were suffering a violent jerk when passing through the points! This matter was referred to the Engineering committee, but little appears to have been done until the subject came up again in February 1886, when 'improvements' (described as 'urgent' by this time) were authorised at an estimated cost of £3,100. The high cost suggests that other work was included in this figure.

During the intervening period, a new trailing crossover had been installed on the east side of the junction, in 1884. This was inspected by Col. Rich for the BOT on 3rd July; he confirmed in his report that the position of the original Worting Junction Signal Box was on the Down side of the line and described it as having 12 levers, with no spares. (Worting Junction will feature more fully in a later article in this series.)

A TIME OF EXPANSION

The limitation caused in having only two running roads on long stretches of the LSWR main line was beginning to cause a considerable problem for the operating department by the mid-1880s. The development of traffic, particularly the volume of passenger services required to convey an ever expanding populace becoming more accustomed to train travel, played havoc with the engine crews, hard pressed to maintain set diagrams.

Serious delays in train timings, especially in the Up direction, resulted in many late arrivals at Waterloo and led to frustrated complaints from irate passengers. By 1887, there were some 20 main line departures from Basingstoke to London on weekdays. An impression of how the later extension of the quadrupling to Worting Junction facilitated improvements can be gained from the 1910 time-table, which shows 20 stopping and 10 passing expresses on Weymouth or West of England workings. Increases in local services, such as those to Hurstbourne and Fullerton in 1885 and the commencement of through North & South working (via Oxford) between Newcastle, Birkenhead and the South Coast (in 1902 and 1903 respectively) further added to the pressures being experienced at Basingstoke, which was rapidly becoming a serious bottleneck.

Simultaneously with this growth in the latter part of the 19th century, the town of Basingstoke itself was expanding rapidly as prosperity grew. The establishment of several industries changed the basic focus of the area away from agriculture, so long the mainstay of the town's economy. From 1870, the population grew rapidly - a 20% increase to 6,681 in

The transition from old to new is clearly shown here. The earlier station house is partly demolished, whilst in the foreground the new and much larger building takes shape. The photograph was almost certainly taken on the same occasion as the one shown on page 21. A few inquisitive local people make up the scene.

Railway Magazine

1881 was experienced, and a considerable 47% increase over the next two decades; the dawn of the 20th century saw just under 10,000 souls in residence.

NEW AND PROPOSED STATIONS

The period around the turn of the century was a prelude to a decade of considerable activity and transformation in the Basingstoke area. The first steps were taken on 2nd July 1883, when a station was opened at Hook, following successful petitions from the residents of that village and nearby Odiham (theoretically already being served by Winchfield in the eyes of the LSWR).

Their success, the progressive quadrupling of the main line out of Waterloo and the provision of improved facilities, generated interest in some other small communities and requests for local stations were regularly on the agenda for the Board of Directors to consider.

The first evidence of such a request on the fringe of the area was in 1895, when the inhabitants of Steventon (some three miles to the west of Worting) submitted a resolution that they be provided with a station. The LSWR were not unreceptive and ordered in May of that year that 'plans and estimates for a station be prepared'. It was sub-sequently reported, on 11th December, that the estimated cost of this provision would be £7,570, but it was decided not to proceed further. A second request from the disappointed residents' in July 1901 met with a negative response from the company.

It was reported in January 1903 that the LSWR were considering a suggestion for a station at Winklebury, between Basingstoke and Worting Junction; this would probably have been located close to the junction with the then recently opened light railway to Alton. However, this did not materialise, and no further reference in the Minute Books has been found.

The Parish Council at Old Basing were also active in their campaigning for a station, having first proposed the idea in January 1897, but without success. Another concerted push in March 1903 even managed to enlist the support of Wyndham Portal, the prominent LSWR Director. Alas, their resolution 'That there should no longer be delay in providing a convenient station on the LSWR at Old Basing' met with a cold rebuff by the company.

THE REDEVELOPMENT BEGINS

The LSWR Directors appear to have been considering the future enlargement of their Basingstoke station as early as 1883, as a reference has been found (dated February of that year) concerning the postponing of the provision of a new siding and cattle pens pending 'possible station redevelopment'. A further reference, in the *Hants & Berks Gazette* during December 1882, indicates that the District Council had noted the company's pursuance of land acquisition contiguous to the railway, and 'assume improvements' will be forthcoming'. This belief was further consolidated some twelve months later when it was reported (on 9th January) that a letter had been sent to Basingstoke Town Council informing them that the company was seeking Parliamentary powers for land purchases in connection with the remodelling of the station and surrounding area.

The first practical move in the progressive quadrupling of the main line westwards from Woking appears to originate with a letter from the LSWR Engineer on 19th July 1893, asking the Board for instructions as to the preparation of plans for the lands that would be required for the widening between Woking and Worting Junction. Interestingly, when the resulting plans were submitted on 9th October, they were based upon four running lines between Basingstoke and Worting, but only three between Woking and Basingstoke. It was stated that the purchase of 50 acres of land would be required to enable the work to be carried out.

The Directors, unsure that three lines would be able to accommodate future traffic levels, wisely requested that their engineer provide plans for four running lines throughout. Revised submissions were considered in November. These included reconstruction of the stations at Farnborough, Fleet, Winchfield and Basingstoke (though, surprisingly, not Hook). They were then referred to the Traffic Committee for consideration. Approval was given on the basis that 'any lands which may be necessary in view of possible requirements in the future between Woking and Worting Junction to be purchased as opportunity affords'. The matter came up again in October 1894, when further plans (including a 'flyover' junction at Worting) were considered. The LSWR decided to keep the widening 'under review', but would be applying for the necessary powers to purchase the land required (now some 94 acres) in the next Parliamentary session. However, for some reason, the application did not go forward until early 1897, when notices for widening and other improvements appeared in the Parish of Basing (and others) in November 1896.

THE WIDENING UNDER WAY

Work on quadrupling the short section from Basingstoke to Worting Junction was authorised as early as May 1894, with estimates to be prepared. Construction, incorporating the new flyover (taking the Up line from Southampton over the Salisbury and West of England line) commenced in the spring of 1896. This was facilitated, it would appear, by the fact that little additional land was required for this section; the LSWR already owned sufficient to be able to proceed with the works. The *South Western Gazette* of October 1896 highlighted the progress being made:

'The object of this widening is to do away with the junction of the Southampton and Exeter lines at Worting, or rather to remove this junction to Basingstoke. Later on the widening will be continued on through the station and on to Woking.

'The work now in hand commences just west of Basingstoke Station and terminates about a half mile west from Worting junction. The bulk of the widening is on the Up line side and includes several cuttings and embankments. The embankments are considerably heavier than the cuttings and consequently this excess is being obtained by making the Worting cutting much wider than would otherwise be necessary. In this cutting some 80,000 cubic yards will be removed.

'The geological formation consists of chalk throughout and this is being removed at a rapid rate (about 4000 cubic yards per week) by a steam navvy, not perhaps inappropriately christened a "steam devil" by the villagers. The bridges to be built are eight in number, one at Worting is of peculiar construction, advantage being taken of the curious design of the old bridge by raising and strengthening the wings of this bridge to form the new abutments. The superstructure will be of iron and steel.

'Near Worting junction the new Up Southampton line will cross the Exeter lines at a very acute angle. Although the span measured on the square is twenty six feet, the skew span is 140 feet. The abutments will be of Bishops Waltham bricks and the girders of the "Whipplc-Murphy" type. These girders will be 150 feet in length and 15 feet deep in the centre. The operations necessitated the removal of the signalman's cottages at Worting junction; new ones to take their place have been erected. Although the work was only started in the latter part of April last, quite a record progress has been made; four of the bridges are complete and the line is finished to formation level for about one and a half miles'. The new facilities were recorded as being brought into use on 20th May 1897.

The contract for widening from Woking to Basingstoke was awarded to Messrs. Lucas and Aird. The *Railway Magazine* of December 1899 recorded that 'Work has begun on widening the line from Woking to Basingstoke. Plans for enlarging Basingstoke station have been prepared and all the necessary land purchased'. The contract was actually divided into two sections: Woking to Winchfield, and Winchfield to Basingstoke. The work was to be undertaken simultaneously under the direction of two of the LSWR Company's Engineers; the Engineer appointed on the

latter section was Mr. A.J. Fisher.

Available information suggests that the *Railway Maga-zine* was somewhat dilatory in its reporting, as work was apace many months before. In the Basingstoke area, several preliminary steps were taken. The most significant was the authorised diversion of Reading Road, to enable a new steel overbridge to be constructed as a replacement for the original structure. This was undertaken in 1897 by Messrs. Lucas and Aird at an estimated cost of £5,200, the *Hants & Berks Gazette* intimating in May that 'a new bridge will shortly be thrown across the metals in place of the existing feature'.

To cope with the anticipated increase in traffic following the widening, the provision of several new block sections between Woking and Basingstoke were approved in May 1897. In the Basingstoke area, these were at Newnham Cutting (between Hook and Old Basing), Basing Castle, also referred to as Old Basing (between Old Basing and Basingstoke), Barton Mill (approaching Basingstoke), Winklebury (between Basingstoke and Worting Junction) and Battledown (at the actual divergence of the South-ampton and Salisbury lines). Three years previously, break-section signal boxes had also been provided between Worting and Micheldever at Wootton, Steventon and Litchfield (renamed Roundwood in 1950) at an estimated cost of £850.

Following successful trials at Grateley in 1901, the LSWR decided to employ low pressure pneumatic sig-nalling between Woking and Basingstoke. (Again this signalling system will be covered separately in a future issue.)

By the middle of 1900, work was progressing well on the Winchfield to Basingstoke section, although the contractors were pressing the LSWR for an increase in the agreed price for earthworks. Their claim for 1d. per yard for leads of ¾ to 1 mile, and 3d. per yard for 1 to 2 mile leads came before the Directors in August; eventually, a settlement was reached at ¾d. and 1½d. per yard respect-ively. There may be an indication here that work on the formation was proving more difficult than envisaged, possibly in the area around Basing, where the long embankment had caused problems some sixty-two years previously.

The contractors were not the only concern to the South Western Company at this time. It was found necessary to negotiate with the Basingstoke Canal Company regarding the temporary closures to the waterway in order to carry out widening of the formation of the railway. Eventually this matter was resolved (in April 1902), whereby the Canal Company were to be paid £1,000 per month so long as the canal was closed, with a minimum payment of £4,000. In addition, the LSWR would arrange for the transit of traffic between those points where the canal was stopped.

With the steady progress of earthworks, which had now reached eastwards beyond Hook, the matter of the new station at Basingstoke fell before the Directors. The LSWR Engineer had prepared plans entailing a major rebuilding of the passenger facilities, with new extensive goods yards on both sides of the line to the west of the station. The Down side yard (incorporating a large goods shed) was intended to be 'local', and serve the requirements for the town and surrounding area. The extensive sidings on the Up side were for handling the considerable interchange traffic with the GWR. A new three-road engine shed completed the proposed facilities, which would sweep away the old station area, and transform the scene beyond recognition. The Board, having satisfied themselves of the need for this mammoth redevelopment, approved the proposals in August 1900, at a cost estimated at £117,500. It should be borne in mind that this cost would almost certainly be exclusive of land which, along with costs of demolition of property in the station area, would have been charged to the widening works account.

The contract for the work to the west of the station was awarded to Joseph Firbank under the same agreement as his then current contract schedule with the LSWR for works at Salisbury. The preparation of tenders for the station buildings was not finalised until 1903.

During January 1901, the *Hants & Berks Gazette* reported on the progress of the widening, indicating that the Basingstoke to Winchfield section was the 'further advanced'. The short tunnels at Hook and Winchfield were being removed altogether, the latter requiring a road diversion and the construction of a road bridge, some fifty feet above rail level in height. The *Gazette* also recorded that 'The extra platforms necessitated by the four-track way are practically completed at Winchfield and Hook. At Old Basing Signal Cabin, two and a half miles from Basingstoke, one of the extra two tracks is actually laid and ballasted'.

It was reported to the Directors in April 1902 that the second link in the widening scheme, the 9½

The new works underway on the downside showing the road leading up to the station. Several buildings had to be purchased and demolished to provide for the planned facilities. These included the public house (seen here on the left) as reported in February 1904 and several cottages, although five of these were later reprieved as not being required and were later repaired for £39. 10s. by Mr. Mundy a local builder. By this time the station master was Mr E. Prince, who arrived from a similar post at Weybridge in August 1902. He later rose to Station Superintendent at Waterloo by 1917.
                                                                Railway Magazine

miles from Elvetham (between Fleet and Winchfield) to Basingstoke East signal box, would be ready to be brought into use on 1st June. In the event, the actual opening (including the new, enlarged station at Hook) was brought forward to 25th May to cope with the anticipated rush of passengers to view the Coronation of King Edward VII. The extent of the works in the station area still prevented the uninterrupted use of the four running lines between Worting Junction and the East signal box; that task continued for some further months.

PART 2 of BASINGSTOKE dealing with the rebuilding of the station will feature shortly.

Below: Peter Holt collection

LONDON & SOUTH WESTERN RAILWAY.

London District Superintendent's Office, Waterloo Station.

Special Notice No. S.421.L.D.   TO ALL CONCERNED.   9th May 1918.

VACANCY.

(2).

Position.	Station.	Rates of Pay		Qualifications.
		Min.	Max.	
Signalman	Basingstoke (West Box)	27/0	29/0	Thorough knowledge of Signalling.

(F.S.15,119).

TODAY, THURSDAY, 9TH MAY.

(3). NORTH EASTERN CO'S TROLLEY NO. 77,488, LOADED, DARLINGTON TO BROCKENHURST, will work in ordinary goods trains as under :-

Nine Elms ... ...   dep 10-8 pm
Woking   ... arr 12A14am dep   5A30 am   "A" On Friday, 10th May.
Micheldever   arr 9A29am dep   2A15 pm

THE 10-8 PM GOODS NINE ELMS TO GUILDFORD, TODAY, THURSDAY, 9TH MAY, MUST NOT PASS THROUGH WOKING STATION ON THE DOWN LOCAL LINE.
THE TROLLEY IS WIDE OF GAUGE AND MUST BE ATTACHED NEXT INSIDE THE REAR GUARD'S VAN OF THE GOODS TRAIN CONCERNED.
LOADING DOCK ROADS AND SIDINGS ADJOINING OTHER STRUCTURES TO BE AVOIDED.   CAREFUL HANDLING IS ESSENTIAL.   (J).

(4). NORTH EASTERN CO'S TROLLEY NO. 77823, LOADED, ST. PETERS TO SOUTHAMPTON, will work in ordinary goods trains as under :-

Basingstoke ... ...   dep 6-30 pm
Micheldever ... ... arr 7-8 pm   dep 12A17 am
Southampton Docks   arr 1A16am   "A" On Friday
                                                19th May.

THE TROLLEY IS WIDE OF GAUGE AND MUST BE ATTACHED NEXT INSIDE THE REAR GUARD'S VAN OF THE GOODS TRAIN CONCERNED.
LOADING DOCK ROADS AND SIDINGS ADJOINING OTHER STRUCTURES TO BE AVOIDED.
MR TANCOCK, SOUTHAMPTON, to advise me immediately the trolley has been unloaded and is ready to be sent away, when instructions for disposal will be given.

(5). THE 7-15 PM COMMON USER TRAIN SOUTHAMPTON DOCKS TO BRENT will run and terminate at Barnes with 44 wagons for the G.N.Co.

THE 9-50 PM COMMON USER TRAIN SOUTHAMPTON DOCKS TO KEW EAST will run to Nine Elms via Main Line.

MISSED OPPORTUNITIES 1

In the first of an occasional series of *'Might Have Beens'*, Peter Bailey examines the LSWR design for the Urie 4-8-0

When Drummond died quite suddenly in 1912 he was succeeded, not by an incomer from another railway, but by his friend and colleague, Robert Urie. For some years Urie had been Works Manager at Eastleigh. He was therefore well aware of the motive power situation on the South Western and one wonders whether there had been exchanges between the two men about the way in which policy was progressing with regard to the larger locomotives.

Both Adams and Drummond had left the company well provided with small and medium sized engines. If one excludes the double-singles, there was little that could be said in criticism of the large numbers of 4-4-0s and 0-6-0s which handled the majority of main line workings or of the 0-4-4 and 0-6-0 tank locomotives which looked after the short haul services and yard work. That they were still doing so nearly forty years later says it all.

The weakness was in the provision of really large locomotives. Drummond had failed badly in his attempts to provide a competent, powerful 4-6-0. Robert Urie set out to correct this situation, by providing three classes which, in many respects, provided the template for locomotives of that wheel arrangement for the remaining years of steam. The South Western beat even the Great Western in the provision of 4-6-0s with a range of wheel diameters between five and a half and six and a half feet, whilst the standard British Railways mixed traffic 4-6-0s were the swan song of a concept which had been dominant for over forty years.

Significant to the notes which follow was the first of these, the H15. The first batch was a direct replacement for a stillborn Drummond six foot 4-6-0, class K15. Incidentally, had Drummond lived, the H15 classification would have gone to an 0-8-0 goods locomotive, another design which never saw the light of day.

Like many other enthusiastic steam engineers, Robert Urie flexed his wings and set his team to work on schematic drawings for a wide range of locomotives. Amongst these was the 4-8-0. From the limited information which has been published, certain things are clear. It would have followed fairly close on the heals of the first batch of H15s and carried the same, very large, five foot six inch diameter boiler. This, one suspects

from its dimensions and appearance, drew to some extent on the design Drummond had used for his earliest 4-6-0s. It was a parallel boiler although, a few years later, it was to dawn on Urie's team that water was most effectively heated at the firebox end and that at least the same efficiency could be achieved from a lighter boiler, which tapered inwards at the forward end. This was the one which graced the N15s and S15s and later H15s.

Another Drummond feature, perpetuated in the early Urie 4-6-0s, was the large cutaway in the side sheets of the cab. Looking at its known features, one is led to conclude that the 4-8-0 would probably have appeared as early as 1913 or 1914. Unsurprisingly, in view of the structural weakness of the Drummond "water cart", as on the first H15s, the tender was pure Urie. Other features, two outside cylinders with Walschaerts gear and a high running plate for ease of access, also spoke of commonality with the H15. The 4-8-0 appears to have been a well thought out design and there is no reason to suspect that it would have been any less successful than the 4-6-0 which, in its fully developed form, was such a useful workhorse and put the Drummond engines completely in the shade.

The boiler would have shared dimensions with the H15, but the cylinders would have been bored ½ inch larger, at 21 ½ inches. The driving wheels would have been smaller in diameter at five feet and one inch. Thus the tractive effort would have worked out at 32.463lbs, a hefty figure for the day, suggesting the ability to move a substantial load.

So why was the design not developed into an actual locomotive? Quite simply, on a system where passenger was king and freight far less important than on other railways, there would have been too little work for it to do. The far more versatile S15, which followed a few years later, was a more sensible proposition.

There is no doubt that the 4-8-0 was designed purely as a freight engine. The six foot H15s and five foot seven S15s struggled to maintained express passenger speeds, so the smaller wheels of the eight coupled locomotive would have precluded serious passenger work of any kind. It would have been happy between forty and fifty miles per hour, so would have coped more than adequately with fitted van trains to and from Southampton Docks, whilst its great power would

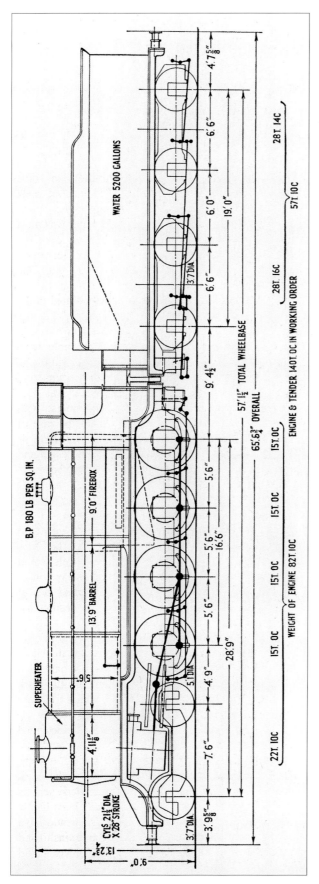

have been ideal for heavy freight workings over the banks beyond Salisbury. For these duties, a class of ten locomotives may, perhaps, have been justified. It is unlikely that there would have been work for more. Certainly they would have been painted in goods colours, holly rather than sage green, with the black borders and simple dividing line which gave such a dignified elegance to freight locomotives on the LSWR. In due course they would have appeared in the Southern's goods livery of black with green lining and ultimately in unlined black.

They may or may not have qualified for smoke deflectors. Certainly not on the grounds of speed, although one is tempted to conclude that, once the Southern had decided what sort of deflectors it liked the look of, these were as much a matter of style as of substance, so that they were fitted to anything large. Whether they enhanced the appearances of any of the Company's locomotives is a matter of opinion.

The drawing shows the locomotive lettered for the LSWR and carrying the number 530, This number is plucked out of the air, although it was ultimately given to a much smaller 5 foot 1 inch goods engine. It would have been a slap in the eye for the Jubilee originally carrying that number, which would either have been renumbered, or duplicated as 0530!

A final thought. Twenty years later Maunsell again considered a freight 4-8-0. It would have related to the Lord Nelson class in much the same way as the Urie design did to the H15. That one bit the dust too, for lack of suitable trains to pull. For those of us who love things Southern, fate, perhaps, dealt us a double blow.

Location unknown - any guesses, but not a lot to go on?

34085, the light engine, seen outside Eastleigh Works on 9th January 1950 and two days before official records reveal it entered works for a Heavy-Intermediate repair which included fitting a new right hand cylinder. At this stage the engine had run a total of 45,725 miles from new and before being released back into traffic on 24th February 1950 it was also repainted in BR livery. It will be noted from the photographs that nameplates had not been fitted to either machine at this stage, whilst both engines involved were just 13 months old. Also 34085 was destined to be rebuilt in June 1960 34084 never was. Each would survive in traffic until 1965, being withdrawn within a month of each other in the autumn of that year. (At that time I also bought the smokebox numberplate from 34085 for 5/-, wish I still had it!)

VICTORIA: 9ᵗʰ DECEMBER 1949

A SAD MISTAKE.

On 9ᵗʰ December 1949 around 6.42 pm on a dark but fine winter's evening an accident occurred on the outskirts of Victoria station (Eastern Section) between the up 'Golden Arrow' (4.55pm from Dover) and a light engine which had passed the Up Relief Signal at Danger.

The facts are simply told. The incoming train, consisting of ten vehicles and hauled by 34084 - later named '605 Squadron' - approached under clear signals and had been signalled into Platform 8 when, for reasons which will be explained in a moment, instead of stopping as it should a light engine, 34085 - later named '501 Squadron' - continued past a danger signal and came into sideways collision with the engine of the 'Golden Arrow'. At the time the 'Golden Arrow' was legitimately crossing from the up main to up relief lines and the collision was between the left hand side of the 34084 and right hand side of 34085.

The momentum of the collision, even though it occurred at no more than about ten mph, was sufficient to tilt the light engine, 34085, over to an angle of 35° and in so doing it fouled the Down Local Line of the Central Section at which point the 6.40 pm eight-coach electric from Victoria to West Croydon was passing under clear signals. (Other reports have referred to this being an East Croydon bound service, but this is incorrect.)

Panelling of the electric train was damaged and thirty-one windows were broken with eight passengers from this service slightly injured, mainly suffering from cuts. Three railwaymen, the driver and fireman of the light engine and Guard Denny of the electric were also slightly injured.

HOW?

How it happened is easy to understand. The light engine was approaching the terminus, with its intended duty to back onto the coaches of the 'Golden Arrow' and pull these away for servicing at Battersea, once the train had arrived and disgorged its passengers. On board the light engine was Driver P. Sheehan, a man with 25 years railway service, the past 15 months of which had been spent as a driver, but three and a half years before this as a Passed Fireman. All of his railway service had been spent at Stewarts Lane. He had been on the same duty since the start of the week. The only difference on this occasion was that his regular Fireman was not present. Instead he was accompanied on the footplate by Passed Cleaner A. E. Turner, aged just 16½.

This crew had already worked an empty stock train from Victoria to Stewarts Lane earlier during their shift. On this occasion they had been due to leave Stewarts Lane for Victoria at 6.30 pm, but for reasons not explained were five minutes late. Even so it would not have mattered, as the 'Golden Arrow' was itself 12 minutes late from its scheduled 6.30 pm arrival time and, with a running time of seven minutes for the light-engine from Stewarts Lane to Victoria, the two workings would likely arrive simultaneously – as indeed did.

But this still would not have mattered provided the signals were obeyed; the official enquiry verified the signalling equipment was working correctly and likewise the signalling layout. Similarly there was no suggestion of any outside event or other failure being a contributory factor.

As it is also known, the approach to Victoria is on a steep downhill gradient, curved in places. The steepest part of the descent is as great as 1 in 62, although this eases to 1 in 290, after which it finally becomes level within the station itself. Driver Sheehan was thus occupied with controlling the brake and, although he observed a yellow indication for his engine and reduced speed accordingly, he admitted he did not see the indication of the Up Relief Line Signal at Danger as he was on the 'wrong' side of the footplate. Instead, he admitted he mistakenly believed he read the subsidiary ground signal in the 'off' position and was then occupied in looking for the next ground signal, when he was overtaken by the 'Golden Arrow' and the collision occurred. (Subsequent tests revealed that signal 151, the one passed at danger by 34085, was only visible from the driver's side of the engine at a distance of 39 yards. However, from the right hand side of the cab the same signal was visible from about 150 yards.)

Speed was not an issue although observation was, whilst what was described as, perhaps, a very slight mist was noticed by some watchers later. The 'Golden Arrow' was approaching the terminus at about 10 mph, the light engine about 5 mph. The speed of the electric set was the greatest and it had already accelerated to around 30 mph.

The fact that Driver Sheehan was on the left side of the light engine, 34085, meant that, allied to the position of signal 151 and the bulk of the engine casing, he was leaning out as much as he could but its, bulk

27

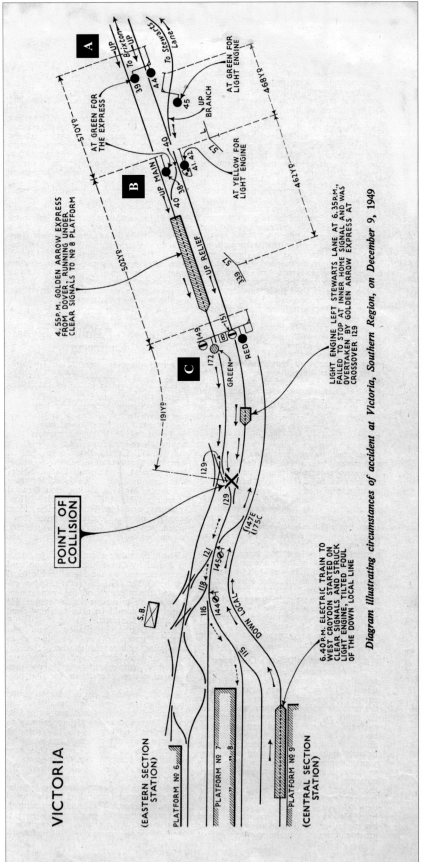

Diagram illustrating circumstances of accident at Victoria, Southern Region, on December 9, 1949

	Up Main	Up Relief
A – Second Outer Homes (3-aspect)	No 39	No 45 (Up Branch to Up Relief)
Intervening Distance	570 yards	468 yards
B – Outer Homes (3-aspect)	No 38	No 41
Intervening distance	502 yards	502 yards
C – Inner Homes with platform route indicators	3-aspect running signal worked by 8 levers. (No 172 for No 8 platform.) Flood-lit disc. Subsidiary No 149.	3-aspect running signal, worked by 8 levers. Flood-lit disc Subsidiary No 151.

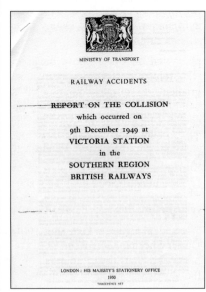

MINISTRY OF TRANSPORT

RAILWAY ACCIDENTS

REPORT ON THE COLLISION

which occurred on

9th December 1949 at

VICTORIA STATION

in the

SOUTHERN REGION

BRITISH RAILWAYS

LONDON : HIS MAJESTY'S STATIONERY OFFICE
1950
THREEPENCE NET

The only view of 34084, the engine from the 'Golden Arrow'. This and sister engine 34083 were both kept by Stewarts Lane in pristine condition, especially for the 'Golden Arrow' workings. Recorded here outside the front of Eastleigh Works on 9th January 1950, the engine was officially classified as receiving a Heavy Intermediate Repair between 6th January and 10th March. This involved a new left hand cylinder, alterations (possibly platework?) to the front end, new horizontal (frame) stretchers, a new main steam pipe and a new boiler, No 1277, was also fitted. The latter item was necessary due to the rate at which the boiler emptied itself following the shearing of a mud plug in the accident and as described in the text. The cumulative mileage to this time was 42,622. Curiously, the official record refers to the repair referred to as having been carried out at Brighton, although the engine is definitely depicted here at Eastleigh. It is of course possible that it may have been photographed here and then moved to Brighton for the work.

prevented anything like a clear view. He admitted he was reluctant to leave control of the brake on the gradient. In circumstances such as this the Fireman would normally assist in calling out the indication of a signal which was difficult for the driver to see, but Turner's lack of experience in this area did not help. Indeed, at the time of the accident Passed Cleaner Turner was stated to be attending to the fire and water levels and confirmed he did not see any of the signals.

WHY?

The blame then must reluctantly be passed to Driver Sheehan. The issue of his reluctance to leave the brake and cross the footplate to observe the indication of the signal was brought up at the enquiry, what was not

asked was why Sheehan had not instructed Turner to observe the signal concerned. It would not have absolved the Driver from the overall responsibility nor for confirming the indication himself, but it might have helped. This is perhaps all the more difficult to understand as the crew had worked in and out of Victoria earlier on the same shift. Indeed, it appears there is no record of any conversation between the Driver and Fireman beforehand.

THE AFTERMATH

Not surprisingly, there was both considerable disruption to traffic and damage to equipment and stock. 34084 and its Pullman train came to a stand 85 yards from the point of collision. So far as the engine from the

The remains of the cab of 34085, which, as mentioned by the Inspecting Officer, "…was demolished". The pseudo Southern Railway livery, although with BR wording on the tender, will be noted.

'Golden Arrow' was concerned, damage started at the left cylinder and the associated area. The main frame was also buckled, whilst the mud hole plug on the left hand corner of the firebox was ripped off, which allowed boiler water and steam to escape. This happened faster than Fireman Russell of the 'Golden Arrow' was able to throw out the fire and in consequence a fusible plug melted. There was also considerable damage to the casing and cab along the same side. (The consequential damage to the firebox necessitated a replacement boiler being fitted when later repairs were carried out.)

34085, the light engine, suffered similar damage but to the right hand side. Again the cylinder was damaged as was the motion, whilst Lieutenant Colonel G. R. S. Wilson, the Inspecting Officer for the Ministry of Transport noted: "…the side of the cab was demolished".

Of the 'Golden Arrow' train there was superficial damage to the first two vehicles, "baggage and container trucks" and also to the two leading Pullman cars, on their left sides just above underframe level. Some axle boxes were also broken. The remaining six Pullman vehicles were undamaged. No other details are given in the report as to the identity of the rolling stock involved, nor of the unit numbers of the electric units.

Damage to the electric sets commenced with the third coach of the first set and included having the butterfly valve from the communication cord at the end of the vehicle ripped off. This, of course, immediately applied the brakes, although Motorman Chapman similarly applied the brakes a few seconds later. His train came to rest under Ebury Bridge, some 185 yards from the initial point of collision between 34085 and the third coach of his train. He did not witness the accident, but did hear the noise behind him.

As mentioned earlier, the light engine was by now tilted at an angle so as to come into contact with the electric unit and in this form it continued to scrape the electric set for the remainder of its length until the electric came to rest. Most of this damage appears to have been caused by the right hand smoke deflector of 34085. (Views of 34085 after the accident show this

The front end of 34085 Damage was stated as: "broken right hand cylinder casing, motion, cab side, smokebox pierced." As with 34084, this was another Stewarts Lane engine.

right hand smoke deflector missing, which means it may well have been ripped off as a result.)

The derailment of 34085 also caused a heavy short circuit and current was cut off to the conductor rails by the circuit breakers at the Victoria sub-station. As per routine they were immediately closed again but in response to a message to the sub-station from Victoria Eastern Signal Box, the current was completely cut off within half a minute of the accident. The passengers from both services were detrained onto the ground with the assistance of railway staff. First Aid was given by railway staff on the ground and also by the station First Aid post.

RESTORATION

Understandably there was considerable disruption to the Eastern Section side of the station and to Central Section lines to a lesser degree. The down local line was restored to use by 11.00 pm whilst 34085 was re-railed by the combined efforts of the Nine Elms

and Bricklayers Arms cranes by 4.40 am the next day. Following necessary track repairs all lines were back in operation by 8.40 am on 10th December, just 14 hours after the accident. Both engines would have had to be towed away following the collision, although there is a surprising lack of further information concerning their movements, with the only located item being in the January 1950 issue of the *Railway Observer,* where it was noted that: "On the following day, 34085 minus tender was standing on the through road between platforms 9 and 10 on the suburban side of the Central Section station in company with two 0-6-0s, 31575 (C class) and 33038 (Q1 class)." Possibly one of these was later used to haul the engine away as, even then, it was unlikely the railway would wish to have any obvious visible reminder of the incident.

CONCLUSION

Despite the reference to Driver Sheehan having been on a similar duty for the preceding four days, the

Above - *Full sideways view of 34085, unfortunately no views appear to have survived of the actual accident scene and likewise the electric units involved. Similarly there is just the one view of 34084 - as seen on page 29. According to Bradley the crews of both steam engines observed the danger, but it too late to avoid a collision This, though, is not borne out in the official report. Bradley also refers to the electric set involved as travelling at 35 mph, slightly faster than that stated in the official report. BR estimates give the total cost of damage both on site and to the locomotives and rolling stock involved as at £13,800. Sister engine 34084 was also to be involved in the spectacular Hither Green derailment of 20th February 1960, when it rolled down an embankment.*

report was not totally clear as to the circumstances Sheehan had faced approaching Victoria on these previous occasions. His recollection of the past events was described by the Inspecting Officer in his report as "vague". Sheehan did perhaps think that on two of these occasions the 'Golden Arrow' was already in the platform, but he also commented he would expect to be held at the signal anyway. (Nowhere in the report is there any suggestion either that his regular Fireman was interviewed to see if he could recall the previous four days.)

With no evidence to support equipment failure or other cause, the Inspecting Officer had no alternative but to lay the blame solely with Driver Sheehan on 34085. (D L Bradley in his work *Locomotives of the Southern Railway Part 2*, page 76, refers to the fact that the driver of 34085 had misread the signals and believed he was in fact travelling on the up main rather than the up relief. Accordingly, the clear indications he saw were

in fact for the inbound 'Golden Arrow'. This mitigation is not referred to in the official report.) This was also the first occasion in 25 years when any incident had been recorded against Sheehan and he was reported as being regarded by his superiors as a steady man. Details of Sheehan's subsequent career are not reported and the conclusions of Lieutenant Colonel Wilson were to the effect that he could not accept that Sheehan could not cross the footplate for even a brief moment even though he was correct not to trust his young and inexperienced Fireman. In mitigation Wilson did acknowledge that Sheehan had not made any attempt to excuse his failure and the conclusion was that the accident was due to a lack of concentration at a critical moment. Indeed Sheehan admitted that since the accident he had "… racked his brains through and through…" and could not explain how his mistake had arisen.

With thanks to John Wenyon, Tim Stubbs, and Alan Butcher.

...and speaking of Bulleids, this of course is how they should look even if seen here in rather grimy condition. 34103 'Calstock' pulls away from Reading West heading south on an inter-regional working sometime in the early 1960s. Allocated to Bournemouth, the engine has no doubt worked north to Oxford earlier in the day and is now on its way back to home territory. The first vehicle is clearly a Bulleid restaurant car, the Southern Region keen not to loose its own vehicles northwards and so the attachment was made at Oxford.

Brian Davis collection

...and which also leads us in rather neatly, if sadly to the article over the page...

'WITHER THE SOMERSET AND DORSET'

The sad, and at times downright deceitful way, closure of the S & D was achieved.

Paul Heathcote

In life I think we can all relate to various events that have had a profound effect on us. It could be a personal happening, good or bad, or professionally, promotion or, at the other end of the scale, perhaps redundancy. I use the latter word deliberately in relation to what is to follow.

Even in the journey through this railway hobby of ours there can be similar milestones; perhaps the discovery of a new photograph, or a book on a favourite subject. Indeed despite the veritable plethora of new material appearing on the shelves there still seem to be new surprises that abound.

Such an event occurred quite recently when I was passed a sheaf of papers appertaining to the S & D. This was in the form of a British Railways file from the Western Region covering, in detail, primarily a twelve month period from 1959, but with odd comments from earlier and later, and inevitably one of many hundreds, probably thousands, that the nationalised railway produced. Perhaps the term 'generated' would be more appropriate, with every individual subject seemingly the subject of a similar file of papers.

"Did you say Western Region?" I hear you ask, and indeed the answer is yes. So the obvious next question has to be, "What relevance is that to *The Southern Way*?" "Elementary, my dear Watson", has to be my reply – and with all due deference to Conan-Doyle. The answer is in the subject of the file, "The Somerset & Dorset Joint Railway, Western and Southern Regions", which, when leafing through its pages literally had that same profound effect referred to at the start of this item.

I should say at this stage that the papers were passed to me in good faith. I have no doubt they were obtained legitimately, probably just one of many thousands of files, eventually put out as refuse and 'rescued' as potentially interesting. The finder was –

well, not anyone whose name has ever appeared in The Southern Way before, and yet despite the passage of time it is probably still appropriate that identities should be protected. So why the 'cloak and dagger' approach? Well, simply that even after 40 years the information may even now be considered to be sensitive. A sad reflection upon a nationalised industry, although it must be said one which was, no doubt, only following the instructions of a Government whose well known catch phrase was, "You've never had it so good". Bah humbug – who had never had it so good, certainly not the potential fortunes of the railway, staff and passengers. (Harold Watkinson was Minister of Transport and Civil Aviation up to October 1959. He was succeeded by Ernest Marples after that date.)

The actual papers I have had loaned to me for some time, always with a response to the owner and a promise that I would read them very soon, or for a change – yes, very interesting. But to be fair neither was strictly accurate. To be honest I had only skimmed through and not found the time to thoroughly disseminate a wad perhaps half and inch thick, but when I did, I could not stop. Here for the first time, in black and white, was documentary proof of the underhand behaviour of the Western Region, in events that would eventually lead to the closure of the Somerset and Dorset, and as there is a definite Southern connection I approached Kevin Robertson with the intention to make public the information once and for all.

Let me say straight away that, in what follows, no personal slur is intended against any of the railway individuals or officers mentioned. This was a time - 1959/60 - when such behaviour whilst not necessarily widespread, was not uncommon either. It has to be said that later 'manipulation' would be seen as justification for closure of a number of lines. In the former South Western area these included Andover to Romsey and the

Opposite page - Scenes around Evercreech Junction. Selecting views to accompany Paul's article was not easy. What does one choose, a live railway, or one that is moribund and melancholy? In the end the choice fell upon an excellent assortment made available to 'Southern Way' from the collection of Paul Hersey. The photographs were taken by his late father, no doubt with a potential modelling project in mind as they display angles and aspects not usually seen. Indeed a train would perhaps seem superfluous. From an written piece, then, where depression cannot be ignored, it is pleasing to think that some good may come out of the photographs seen over the next few pages. The pub is now renamed 'The Silent Whistle'.

Mid Hants at the very least, and there were, no doubt, others.

In trying also to be objective and by not letting emotion run riot, it has to be said that this is just one file on its own. There may well have been others, likewise papers may well be missing, but a genuine attempt has been made to record what is clearly stated in black and white and interpret these without bias. Of what is written there can be no doubt.

In producing, then, what appears to be almost a conclusion at this stage, let it be said that this sort of behaviour clearly had its origins at a very senior level. Someone, somewhere had already made the decision; those names and signatures that appear on the papers were purely the instruments used and against whom blame might now be incorrectly apportioned. They were following policy, not necessarily making it. In the history of the railway network of Britain, in this respect not just the Southern, it is a sad and regretful action which, when judged not just with hindsight, but even contemporaneously, is still a slur on the conscience. It is about time that what is known is made public.

It was stated above that the file located is just one set of papers; indeed, right from the earliest date it is clear there must have been others. Indeed the first reference is on 25th May 1957 in the form of an unsigned memorandum from the 'Office of the Operating Officer' at Paddington, which in its first paragraph states, "This memorandum sets out the Western Region proposals for diverting through passenger trains which now run via the Somerset and Dorset to and from Bournemouth West. For most of the year the only trains involved are the down and up 'Pines Express' but on summer Saturdays the situation is very different and several alternative routes have been examined with a view to 'spreading the trains over these routes'…".

The list of routes is then given, which includes some curious and considerably lengthy alternatives:

1 Barnt Green, Filton Junction, Westbury and Salisbury. (Not stated if from Salisbury this would then involve travel via Fordingbridge or Eastleigh. In the light of later comments it would appear Fordingbridge was the most likely.)
2 Barnt Green, Worcester, Oxford and Basingstoke.
3 Barnt Green, Worcester, Oxford, Newbury and Winchester.
4 Cannock Road Junction, Oxford and Basingstoke.
5 Cannock Road Junction, Oxford, Newbury and Winchester.
6 Wellington (Salop) Oxford and Basingstoke
7 Wellington (Salop) Oxford, Newbury and Winchester

8   Banbury Junction, Oxford and Basingstoke.
9   Banbury Junction, Newbury and Winchester.
10   Barnt Green, Gloucester, Swindon and Basingstoke.
11   Barnt Green, Gloucester, Swindon, Newbury and Winchester
12   Shrewsbury, Hereford, Gloucester, Filton Junction and Salisbury. (Same comment as at number 1 applies.)

An appended note stated, "Although routes 10,11 and 12 entail appreciably extra mileage, they have been considered for one or two trains because of the impossibility of accommodating these trains on the shorter routes." (The memorandum of 25th May states that journey times would only be increased by a maximum of 30 minutes dependent upon the route chosen and with no theoretical increase in some cases. Bearing in mind the planned electrification of the London Midland Region then in the planning process, the reality would probably have been a far greater delay. Nowhere is this mentioned relative to the likely effect upon passengers nor whether they would tolerate increased travel times in a period when competition from road transport was ever increasing.)

However, did the Western Region seriously expect any one of these to be practical? Could anyone at Paddington seriously believe that a route via Hereford was feasible? There can be one conclusion only and that

is as stated in the preamble.

Accordingly, at this stage let us look for a moment at the other issue which is not mentioned here. Why did the Western Region want to close the Somerset and Dorset? The reason given has always been financial. But financial from the perspective of revenue, or financial relative to operation / maintenance? The two headings are very different indeed. From the first perspective, local revenue from the Somerset and Dorset was unlikely to cover operating costs. Indeed the Somerset and Dorset was by this time in the same situation as numerous other routes where the intermediate stations provided more of a social service than a financial return. Dr Beeching would later recognise this and wholesale closure of intermediate stations on main routes took place – but the routes stayed open. What does become visible, although in fairness, this does not appear in the file at this stage, is that *apportioned revenue from passengers travelling in through trains was not attributed to the Somerset and Dorset.* Assuming that to be the case on financial grounds alone a primary school pupil would agree the railway was running at a loss. (The later figures given for cost savings similarly do not include apportioned revenue from through traffic.)

The second factor is similarly stacked against the railway, although it must also be admitted that maintenance was indeed high on this line. The

With reference to this matter; consideration has now been given to the diversion to other routes of all through passenger services at present running over the Somerset and Dorset Line.

Tentative proposals covering alternative routes and train timings so far as concerns the Western Region have been prepared and are set out in a memorandum of which four copies are enclosed herewith.

As you are aware the diversion of all through freight traffic from the S & D Line has already been agreed in principle and a first examination of the economies involved in closing the whole or major part of the Western Region section of the line between Bath (Green Park) and Templecombe Junction shews that a financial advantage of some magnitude would accrue.

You will, therefore, appreciate that I am anxious fully to examine all possibilities of diverting the through passenger services and suggest that, when you have examined this Region's proposals and formulated your own ideas on the subject, a meeting at which the Southern Region would also be represented be held at Paddington to review the whole position.

Part of a letter from Pattison at Paddington to the LMR, 3rd June 1959.

This and previous page. More detail views of Evercreech Junction from the collection of Paul Hersey.

Reference is made on page 40 to a proposed connection between the former Midland and GWR lines near Bath during BR days. A proposal to modify the S & D approach into Bath was certainly not new and was discussed fully in the March 1982 issue of the 'Railway Magazine'. More recently a detailed account will be found in the S & D 'Telegraph'. Both are from the pen of Mike Arlett.

maintenance of tunnels and viaducts was paramount, whilst, operationally, the severe gradients and consequent need for double-heading, plus increasing delays to both road and rail by various level crossings all cause the pounds to start mounting up. Add to this the impracticality of effective cost saving by reducing the number of signal boxes and crossing loops and we have a railway where economy would be difficult to achieve without first involving major investment.

It has been mentioned before that there was never any attempt made to reduce motive power costs by dieselisation, although perhaps for the time in question such a consideration was just too early. What is apparent is that British Railways (and indeed since then the privatised railway) has continually had to 're-invent the wheel'. Lessons learned are either ignored or conveniently forgotten and the flexibility of diesel, even at this stage, was readily known. The Southern had recent experience of its own and the LMR had main line locomotives in service, whilst the Western had the start of a fleet of hydraulics running. Even if the Western Region experience had not been 100% up to that time and the Southern was ignored, does this mean the LMR and ER could not contribute anything? Both at the time were operating a growing fleet of ever more reliable machines.

Indeed it should be said that, up to now, nowhere in the file is there any reference to communication or contact / response from the Southern Region. No doubt Waterloo had its own views and records of the situation as it developed, although with the passage of time it is perhaps unlikely these will be found.

In a continuing attempt to be objective we might also consider further some of the alternative routes. Clearly some of the more rural of these, notably via Barnt Green, or Newbury, or south from Salisbury through Fordingbridge – assuming the latter is the line intended- were themselves already under threat. The fact they were being included was a clear indication that it was already recognised that the preferred main line options were either already at, or close to, capacity, especially if one of these long distance trains missed its booked path and an alternative 'Q' path was now no longer available.

So why suggest these threatened routes in the first place? Here we cannot but draw one inescapable conclusion. *Paddington was determined to divert services off the Somerset and Dorset - at any cost.*

Neither was it just passenger workings that were affected as the next note is from Mr F Pattisson, the Operating Officer at Paddington, to Mr A Turner, the Passenger Services Assistant at the equivalent Operating Officer's Office on the LMR. This is dated 30th June 1959 and includes another bombshell, **"As you are aware the diversion of all through freight traffic from the S & D line has already been agreed in principal and a first examination of the economies involved in closing the whole or major part of the Western Region section of the line between Bath (Green Park) and Templecombe Junction shows that a financial saving of some magnitude would accrue."** The note continued by suggesting a meeting between the WR and LMR at Paddington, at which the Southern Region would also be represented.

Two possible conclusions may thus be drawn; the first is that Waterloo was now involved, although as mentioned above, (we have not had access to any Southern Region paperwork) or, alternatively, that Waterloo was at present being left out in the cold. Whatever the case, any formal minutes that have survived and which may one day be open to scrutiny would be likely to show just a brief comment and not the type of detail now reported.

Matters now move away to Derby and the LMR - who says we cannot be catholic in our approach to the Southern?, where the LMR appears concerned that it would not in fact be possible to fit in the diverted services, in view of the stated intention to move much as many as possible of its own Birmingham trains via Leamington Spa, consequent upon electrification work. Similar letters seeking opinions on closure and any views thereon, were sent to Line Traffic Manager (Operating), Mr G J Aston, at Derby and also the Line Traffic Officer (Operating) at Crewe. The former will feature again shortly.

Then on 20th July there was indeed a private admission from the LMR that any diversion of trains would be likely to affect their own services but with the scornful comment that, "...the inconvenience could be minimised by some extra mileage which could be faced if the economies (*meaning closure of the S & D*) are of some magnitude." I would point out that, up to now, nowhere in the papers is there any mention of the actual saving in pounds sterling that it was estimated would be achieved, but it is to be hoped someone somewhere had indeed done their sums.

The fact such a statement is made - and in a typed note as well - is itself perhaps indicative of general British Railways policy at the time. It might even be summed up as "b****r the passengers and any inconvenience that results, we will get a pat on the back for saving (or making) money", an attitude which appears to prevail today. Profit before service.

However, and this is what makes historical research so rewarding, in the midst of (what the reader will have gathered I refer to as) a sad and unfortunate period in attitude towards the passenger, there were still some who believed in promoting railways as a service, one being the Line Traffic Manager (Operating) Mr G.

> Finally, I cannot too strongly stress that I regard
> this as an opportunity to improve the holiday trains, and
> not merely to close the S.& D. for economy's sake.
> Please do all in your power to force that view on
> Paddington.
>
>   Yours sincerely,

Above - LMR Letter from Aston to others on LMR, 25th July 1959.
Opposite page - Pattison's letter of execution, although as seen he himself was the executioner not the judge.

J. Aston, at Derby.

Mr Aston prepared, or more likely had prepared for him, a response to the Western Region memorandum and, far from accepting blandly the case for closure and consequent increased times for passengers, he had worked out that by better coach balancing allied to tighter engine diagramming it would be possible to substantially reduce the journey time from Sheffield to Bournemouth by running via Banbury compared with times over the existing Somerset and Dorset route. He commented that via Bath the time was currently seven and a half hours and that if the route were to take in Salisbury this would increase to eight hours. Via Banbury, this could be reduced to five and a half hours even if an average speed of only 40 mph was involved.

Here was a man prepared to attempt the best possible, which may well be summed up with the final paragraph of his report, "Finally, I cannot too strongly stress that I regard this as an opportunity to improve the holiday trains, and not merely to close the Somerset and Dorset for economy's sake. Please do all in your power to force that view on Paddington." The impression is therefore that at Derby the dogmatic approach by Paddington to 'closure at all costs' was already recognised.

Before going any further, let us pause for a moment to consider if such acceleration might even have been possible using the Somerset and Dorset route. The answer does not take long to find. A necessary reversal at Bath allied to long stretches of single line working, and double heading on steep gradients meant that even if locomotives fitted with tablet catchers were used, any savings would be notional rather than extensive. Of course main line DMU operation plus track circuiting plus signalling changes would have helped, but the former were hardly available at this stage whilst the latter would have involved much investment.

Following an attempt at a consensus for suitable dates, the all important Paddington meeting was eventually scheduled for Tuesday 24th November 1959. It appears this may have subsequently been brought forward to either the 14th or 18th November, whilst a second meeting on the same subject was held as originally proposed.

Paddington, though, was like a terrier with a rat; it would not let go, and again on the basis of finance made a case that closure would save an estimated £399,000 annually. Interestingly, two things are mentioned in the report which are a puzzle; the first a proposed new £200,000 connection between the LM and Western Region lines at Twerton near Bath, which would allow trains that would otherwise have used the Somerset and Dorset to join the Western Region route at this point and then run via Westbury and Salisbury. The second is a reference to the Southern Region planning an upgrade of the line through Fordingbridge mentioned in the report as, "…referred to later…", although in this case 'later' never came and such a tantalising comment is left hanging.

Indeed Paddington continues with the comment that whilst the Southern Region admits some bridge renewals and repairs will be needed at some stage on the route through Fordingbridge, it is expected to consent to these as an alternative to the costs involved in repairs and maintenance to the Somerset and Dorset. (We may reasonably assume Waterloo did know what view they were allegedly taking - they must - surely…?) So we may reasonably assume that diversion via Fordingbridge was the preferred option for both the Western and Southern Regions east of Salisbury, subject to the latter not considering closure of the Fordingbridge line. (…as indeed it successfully did a few years later. By now also any intention of using the DNS as a diversion appears to have evaporated.)

But behind the scenes it would appear that a new and sinister threat was emerging. Mention has been made already of the tripartite November meeting that took place in late November 1960 between the Western, Southern and Midland Regions, to discuss the line's future. In reality though it had already been decided, for on 8th November David Pattisson at Paddington wrote to A. S. Turner at Euston (the letter was originally supposed to be copied to Waterloo, but this was crossed

B.R.

PICKFORD
General Manager
(Traffic)

R. L. CHARLESWORTH
Commercial Officer

C. W. POWELL
Operating Officer

H. E. A. WHITE, A.M.I.Mech.E.
Running & Maintenance Officer

Telephone
PADDINGTON 7000
Ext.   5-12
Telegraphic Address
HEADTRAF WESRAIL
LONDON, TASN   PH/1187
Telex 24126

BRITISH TRANSPORT COMMISSION

WESTERN REGION
OF
BRITISH RAILWAYS

TRAFFIC HEADQUARTERS

PADDINGTON STATION

LONDON, W.2

8th November, 1960.

Dear Mr. Turner

<u>Somerset and Dorset Line.</u>

   I thought I would send you a personal line in regard
to the various discussions which have taken place, chiefly
between myself and Mr. Sutton in regard to the possibility
of diverting all the through services away from the Somerset
and Dorset line. I had hoped to prepare a report which would
have been agreed by you beforehand so that it represented the
views of the three Regions concerned.

   Due to the pressure of other commitments I have not
been able to progress with this idea as quickly as I had hoped
and I have now been instructed by the Assistant General Manager
that full scale enquiries into the future of the Somerset and
Dorset line, with a view to the early withdrawal of virtually
all the freight and passenger services, must commence at once.
I have therefore had to put the information we have already
collected into memorandum form at very short notice to form
the basis for a final letter to Mr. White and the Director of
Traffic Services.

   I have drawn up the document so that neither the London
Midland nor the Southern Region appear in it to be committed
to any particular line of action. I hope, however, that it
reflects reasonably well the thought which has been given to
the problem up to date. I am enclosing a copy of our memorandum
as I thought you ought to have a copy personally in view of our
close association at the earlier stages of the enquiry.

   With kind regards.

Yours sincerely,

David Patterson

A. S. Turner, Esq.
EUSTON.
R. Sutton, Esq.,
WATERLOO.

out), "…I have now been instructed by the Assistant General Manager that full scale enquiries into the future of the Somerset & Dorset line, with a view to the early withdrawal of virtually all freight and passenger services, must commence at once." Pattisson was firing the arrows, but clearly not making them.

Indeed, such was the haste that a handwritten note was appended to the file, suggesting an application for closure might proceed, with submission to the Area Boards and the Transport Users Consultative Committee by July 1961. Passenger census dates were also already planned, for 2nd January, 18th June, and 13th August 1961. The January date was a Monday, the other two fell on a Sunday. (The fact Sunday traffic on the Somerset and Dorset was nowhere near as heavy as on a Saturday will be noted by the reader.) What was worst of all was a written note stating that a month's ticket revenue would be collected from – January; "The proposed date for closure of the S & D or some part of it is the Summer of 1962."

For its part the Southern Region at this time made two comments, firstly that it could not hope to complete any necessary upgrading of the Fordingbridge line by the summer of 1962 unless definite confirmation of the requirement was received by May 1961. This was to allow locomotives "currently hauling the Pines Express" to use the Fordingbridge route. Additionally the Southern Region representatives commented they would review the position of the remaining southern section of the Somerset and Dorset south of Templecombe if closure north of that point was to definitely go ahead. For its part the LMR stated similarly concerning its own route into Bath.

Not mentioned up to now is the fate of the various branches off the Somerset and Dorset to Burnham, and elsewhere. These were similarly classified by the Western Region as uneconomic and marked for closure, as of course did indeed happen, although it was recognised that some facilitates would have to be retained to serve the collieries around Radstock.

The rest, as they say, is history. Despite the worst efforts of Paddington the TUCC at first refused closure, but then with the underhand measure of removing the through trains as took place in the summer of 1962, it was only ever going to be a matter of time.

Possibly it took this long as Paddington had to wait until the LMR could deal with the increased traffic – speculation here. For its part too, the Southern Region never did upgrade the Fordingbridge line and that closed in 1964.

It would be left to Dr Beeching to execute the final fatal blow, although by that time Paddington had most certainly already made ready the sacrifice.

If there is a question, it is the oft asked one of whether the railways are run for profit or public service, another factor being that in almost every case where a former through route has been disseminated amongst more than one owner / operator closure has followed. The Somerset and Dorset is the classic example, the former Great Central another, likewise the erstwhile MSWJ and DNS lines. Even the Southern Region lines west of Exeter, now no longer serviced from Waterloo, became like uprooted plants without the means of support they once had. Wither then the railway network. Some may forgive, but may we never forget.

I should like to aim at implementation both of the re-routing of the through trains and the withdrawal of the local services as from the commencement of the Summer Service 1962. A somewhat important factor is the position in regard to the maintenance work required on the Running and Maintenance Depot at Bath which I am advised cannot be kept in operation after the Summer of 1962 without considerable expenditure.

Above - Part of the 8th November 1960 report from Paddington copied to both Euston and Waterloo. In the end circumstances would compel the railway to maintain services for a further four years. That, as they say, is history.

Photographs, this and opposite page - Paul Hersey collection.

SANDLING JUNCTION

Two former 8-wheel 'J' type (3rd Brake) Pullman cars, eking out their last years in a new guise at Sandling Junction between Folkestone and Ashford around 1960/1. The actual location was on the down siding at Sandling Junction off the former Hythe line although by this time the line to Hythe had been closed for some years and the former platform was no longer in use. The main line station is in the background.

Visible are Nos P40 and P41, both built by Clayton in 1921 for the SECR and subsequently taken over by the SR and BR. As such they latterly saw service on the 'Thanet Belle' and 'Kentish Belle' services until withdrawn by the Pullman car company in 1960, consequent upon the elimination of steam hauled services on the former South Eastern section.

Between that time the latter part of 1962, these and approximately 18 further vehicles, were sold to BR and converted to the use seen. P40 and P41, latterly designated BR Car Nos 111 and 116 were two of the first three conversions and were on station in either 1960, or certainly at least by the start of the 1961 season. The third vehicle in this first batch was P42, latterly BR Car No 115, which was allocated to a similar use at Wool.

All three were withdrawn on site in 1967. No P42 was scrapped at Wool in the same year. At Sandling, however, P40 and P41 remained in situ for a further five years, no doubt deteriorating all the time and were finally dismembered where they stood in 1972.

Photographs - Martin Dean collection, notes by Antony Ford

MORE FROM THE 'WOODEN BOX'
Salisbury - west end departures

Following on from the feature in the 'Preview' Issue of 'SW', we are pleased to present another selection from material found years ago in a second hand shop and now the property of Taunton Model Railway Group. As before there were no notes accompanying the views although in many respects the views speak for themselves.

To start with then, two N15 class locos from the first batch of the class built at Eastleigh in 1925. Above is No 457 'Sir Belvedere' whilst right in No 449 'Sir Torrre'. Both would appear to be attached to Drummond type tenders from the latter's doomed 4-6-0s. Although undated it is almost certain that the lack of smoke deflectors and 'E' above the number in each case means the views date from the late 1920s or early 1930s.

Two views now of passenger services awaiting departure from the down local, Platform 3. Although duty numbers are shown on the headcode discs, we do not have a record of these for the period, and any attempt to describe the supposed working by relating it to a later period would be fraught with danger. Both engines are now also sporting smoke deflectors whilst the detail differences between No 746 'Pendragon' of 1922, and No 768 'Sir Balin' of 1925 will be noted.

Finally two views of No 747 'Elaine' at rest and then departing from Platform 3. Possibly these were taken on the same day, certainly every detail appears to be identical, the rolling stock, headcode discs / lamp, even the position of the handles on the smokebox door. But is it the same day? The weather may be the clue, seemingly sun and shadows whilst waiting in the platform but certainly the opposite at the time of departure. Of course weather can change, although again was it just a long lay-over? Notice also in the above view the member of the loco crew is in the process of climbing down onto track level.

No 747 was one of the original LSWR 'N15' class being built at Eastleigh in July 1922, one of seven members of the class completed that year. Fitted with a Maunsell superheater in September 1930, the engine was also one of ten members of the class loaned to the LNER between October 1942 and July 1943. The engine remained in traffic until October 1956.

...and speaking of the LNER briefly, which we were and Bulleid Tavern Cars, which we were not, the view opposite turned up recently, courtesy of another friend to 'Southern Way', Alan Butcher. Of the eight pairs of twin cars, this was one of the six pairs loaned to the Midland and, in this case, Eastern Regions during the summer of 1949. Amongst the services they were used on was the 'South Yorkshireman', which may well be the train depicted here. To say they were unpopular with Yorkshire folk (and indeed on all the services they worked north of the Thames at this time), would be an understatement. (See 'Southern Coaches' by Mike King, P159-161.) Unfortunately even under a glass on the original print we cannot be certain as to the identity of the particular vehicle, nor the location. The engine appears to be an 'A1'.

Photograph by Basil Whitworth

Brian Drysdall recalls his days as a youthful train-spotter at St Denys in the last years of the Southern and early BR

MEMORIES OF A YOUNG TRAINSPOTTER

Returning to Southampton from wartime evacuation at Winsor, near Cadnam, in the early part of 1945, it did not take long to find my way to the nearby railway line to watch the trains go by and start collecting names and numbers. This was at the time when parents were not unduly worried about an eight year old going off on his own on a Saturday to indulge in his new found hobby.

The initial vantage point was the 'Horseshoe Bridge' which still links Dukes Road with Adelaide Road. After only a couple of visits, the now demolished footbridge joining Drummond Drive with Priory Road, became the favoured destination for my visits. Again, it did not take too long to find my way to the nearby St. Denys Station which then became my usual trainspotting haunt for three or four years.

In those days, it was quite a busy place. There was a 'head porter' with, at least, four other porters assisting, as well as a permanently manned ticket office. A free ice-cream could be earned on a Saturday afternoon by running errands to a local shop for the porters. However, this 'service' was only available when the 'head porter' was not on duty. In all my visits, I cannot remember ever seeing a station master. At this time, there was also a small W. H. Smith bookstall on number 1 (the up) platform. It was 'manned' by a rather lovely young lady who, on Saturday afternoons, shut up shop and did duty at the terminus station. The bookstall was the usual source for my copies of the Ian Allan ABC's and early copies of 'Trains Illustrated'.

There did not seem to be any very long periods of inactivity, especially on summer Saturdays, with numerous additional holiday services from London to Lymington, Bournemouth, Swanage and Weymouth, many of the last two services travelling via Ringwood, and in some cases, not stopping at Southampton Central. There were also the boat trains that had to be threaded in between the timetabled services and the holiday specials.

Services through St. Denys were very varied. On the Portsmouth line, these were the rather infrequent local services interspersed with the occasional through trains between Portsmouth, Bristol and Cardiff. Probably the highlights of services on this line were the Saturday through trains between Brighton and Bournemouth, Plymouth and Cardiff. Goods traffic on this route was a rarity with only an oil train from Hamble being anything that came near to being regular.

On the main London line, there was always a great variety. There were the approximately hourly expresses to and from Waterloo, through services between Bournemouth, Birkenhead and Newcastle, local trains, mainly originating from Southampton Terminus, to Eastleigh (7d children's return) and occasionally Winchester and Alton. There were also the 'foreign' intrusions from Didcot. Sometimes engines were changed at Winchester Chesil to a Southern locomotive, but at least once a day, a GWR. engine would work through to Southampton Terminus. Goods traffic was also fairly frequent with trains for the docks, Bevois Park or Mount Pleasant yards, or to points further west. There was also a small goods shed just to the north of St. Denys which brought some local traffic to the station.

So with this great variety of traffic, what could one expect in the way of motive power. Almost anything that happened to be around at the time is the answer, with some days bringing real surprises.

The Portsmouth line local services were usually operated by the more antique 4-4-0's like K10's, S11's, L11's and L12's with the T9's and D15's usually on the Bristol and Cardiff trains. As the older locomotives were scrapped, the U's and N's began to take over, but the T9's were not completed supplanted until the advent of the BR standards in the early 1950's. As mentioned earlier, probably the most eagerly awaited trains were the Saturday through services from Brighton. The Bournemouth train was most likely to produce the big surprise. On at least one occasion, an I3, at other times both the J1 and J2 locomotives were used together with an occasional B4X, and as noted in the Preview Issue of *Southern Way*, Brighton atlantics were more regular performers. The Plymouth and Cardiff services did not have quite the same variety, but did produce some Eastern Section U's and U1's with 'Schools' locomotives, now in malachite green, also making some appearances. Later on, some real eye openers began to appear in the form of new 'West Country' class locomotives in their bright malachite green livery. At the time they were un-named and were soon to be followed in the early 1950's by new 4MT 2-6-4T's.

On the main line, the variety was almost infinite. 'Lord Nelsons' and 'King Arthurs' were as frequently seen on the expresses as the new 'Merchant Navys'. However, I cannot remember the 'Bournemouth Belle' being hauled by anything other than a 'Merchant Navy'. Summer Saturdays were a spotter's heaven. The holiday extras would bring almost anything that could move. The Bournemouth / Swanage / Weymouth trains could be headed by the usual express locomotives, not always ably supplemented by H15's, S15's, NI5X's and T14's (Paddleboxes). The Lymington trains were initially hauled by one of the DI5's, and with their demise, it was usually a 'Schools' class locomotive to Brockenhurst.

The GWR. services from Didcot which did not change engines at Winchester Chesil usually produced one of the Collett '2251' class of 0-6-0's, as often as not either 3210, 3211 or 3212, but occasionally a Churchward '4300' would appear. Local trains were usually hauled by either M7's or Tl's, but sometimes such oddities as an A12 (Jubilee) would appear, and on one occasion, the last X6.

Freight traffic was quite heavy at times. The Southern's HI5 and S15 locomotives were usually in charge of the long distance traffic but sometimes one of the less elegant Ql's would appear at the head of the train. The more local freight could well supply a '700',Q, U or N or even one of the ancient '0395s'. There was an occasional local freight originating from Southampton Terminus. This would often stop at the station to drop off two or three, sometimes six, new motorcycles. These would be collected by a gentleman from the Alec Bennett showrooms in Portswood. The mode of transport was a motorcycle and open sidecar which could take just two of the bikes thereby necessitating two or three journeys. After dropping off the bikes, the train would then move forward to shunt at the small goods shed just to the north of the station. This train would usually be in the charge of a tank locomotive of the M7 or T1 classes with the occasional G6.

With Eastleigh Railway Works not far away, the line to Southampton was frequently used for running in locomotives after servicing, and some real strangers could be seen. As often as not, these would be Eastern Section locomotives such as ex-LBSC tank locomotives or ex-SECR. 4-4-0's, or an Eastern Section mogul. There were also occasions when the locomotives that operated in the Southampton Docks arca would go to Eastleigh for servicing and/or repairs, so the sight of a B4 or C14 'hurtling' down the main line back to its normal haunts was a sight to behold.

Not long after the end of the war, the colour was coming back to the railways, and the Southern Railway malachite green certainly brightened up the scene. Some would say the malachite green livery was too garish for locomotives and a return to pre-war olive green would have been preferable. However, a clean, bright locomotive hauling a train of equally colourful coaches was a magnificent sight. At times, it seemed that Eastleigh got a little paint-brush-happy. Apart from the express passenger locomotives, Eastleigh also re-liveried at least four M7's. These were numbers 241, 242, 243 and 244, and as far as I am aware, these were the only ones so treated.

These were the sights observed in mid 1940's onwards. In the 1950's, the standard classes began to take over a great many of the services, with the consequent reduction in variety. Even so, there was still plenty to see, with some surprises for the young trainspotter, who now became a little more adventurous in pursuit of his hobby.

I have been looking for an opportunity to use this view for some time now. Yes, I know it is a '2251' from that 'other railway', but it does fit in with Brian's text very well. However, look more closely. Exactly what is No 3212 doing? Clearly leaving Eastleigh, southwards on what is a train from the DNS, but with at least four Pullman's on the back as well. All the photographers notes record are the train and date, the 12.42 pm from Didcot, Saturday 26th July 1952. Certainly it seems to be struggling a bit in the process. The best we can come up with so far, is an urgent need for the Pullmans at Southampton Docks, 'unless of course YOU know differently.....?'

John Bailey

Accompanying Howard's files were several views of the IOW and whilst the odd one may have been seen before, we know several have not. Many thanks to Dave Hammersley for his work with the captions.

Above - *Isle of Wight Central Railway 4-4-0T No.6 stands in the up loop platform at Newport. Built by Black, Hawthorn & Co. in June 1890, she is pictured soon after delivery and possibly before addition of the number and garter to the side tanks. The train consists of the two Lancaster bogie coaches delivered earlier the same year and a four wheeler inherited from the Isle of Wight (Newport Junction) Railway.*

Below - *IOW Central railcar No 1 probably shortly after delivery in October 1906. A comprehensive history of the locomotive stock on the IOW lines is given in Bradley's book on the subject published by the RCTS in 1982.*

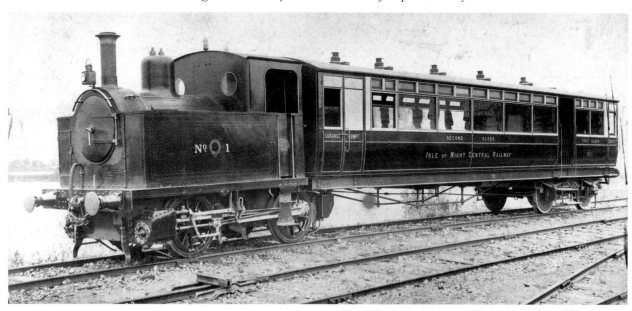

AUDIT TIME ON THE ISLE OF WIGHT
- and a few photographs as well….

Circa 1940/1 the Southern Railway produced an internal set of notes entitled, "A Summary giving particulars of the present Locomotives, Rolling Stock, Stations, Block Systems etc. in the Island, together with some dates concerning the History of the Railways in the Isle of Wight."

Comprising of just 12 sides, the file affords a snapshot of the railway's facilities and equipment and, although unaccredited to any particular individual, *may* have been the work of Hermann Butler – see *Southern Way No 2* of January 2008. This accreditation aspect is discussed more fully later on.

The first few pages, of what initially appears to be a bland set of sheets comprise a resume of the history of the Island railway network, in effect a chronology of openings and proposals, but enlightened with the occasional snippet, perhaps not commonly known. "North Transporter (Medina Wharf) blown along the rails, struck end stop-blocks and collapsed, owing to severe south westerly gale. November 1931 and January 1936."

Following this a page is devoted to the locomotive stock extant at the time, details of which will no doubt already be known to readers of this article.

Afterwards, though, comes information on both the fixed assets and also the rolling stock, including for the first time details of the set formations of the coaches and their allocations in 1940/1. Information for this date is not included in the excellent Oakwood Press volume *Isle of Wight Steam Passenger Rolling Stock* by Maycock and Reed.

Dealing first then with the fixed assets;

CRANES			
Location	**Type**	**Number**	**Capacity**
Medina Wharf	Electric	2	3 Tons Transporter
Ryde Loco	Hand Mobile	1	10 Tons Breakdown
Ryde CME	Hand Mobile	1	2 Tons Yard Crane
Newport Loco	Hand Mobile	1	5 Tons Breakdown
St Helens Quay Hand	Hand	1	10 Tons
St Helens Quay Steam	Steam	1	4 Tons With grab
St Helens Quay Steam	Steam	1	30 Cwts Without grab
Ryde Pier Head	Electric	3	2 Tons For cages
Yarmouth Quay	Hand	1	7½ Tons
Ventnor	Hand	1	5 Tons
Ventnor West	Hand	1	5 Tons (Partly demolished)
Sandown	Hand	1	4 Tons
Shanklin	Hand	1	4 Tons
Hoists and Location			
Ryde CME Works	Hand	1	25 Tons (Note 'a')
Newport Loco	Hand	1	20 Ton (Note 'b')
Ventnor	Hand	2	1 Ton Goods Shed

Note 'a'; Old engine hoist dismantled at Ryde and above new hoist ex Bournemouth fitted 1926.
Note 'b'; Fitted on new site 1939.
Breakdown Appliances;
Newport and Ryde St John's, each – 2 double ramps, 2 traversing jacks, 1 screw jack. At Ryde the equipment was retained in breakdown vans.
Medina Wharf – 2 double ramps, 2 traversing jacks.
Engine Turntable – Bembridge at buffer stops 25'.

WATER TANKS	
Position	Capacity in Gallons
Ryde Pier Head - Loco Supply	2,000
Ryde Pier Head – Boat Supply	3,300
Ryde St John's	5,000
Brading	1,700
St Helens	2,500
Ventnor	5,000
Ventnor West	2,000
Newport – Main Reservoir	10,000
Newport – Loco Supply	7,000
Newport – South Reservoir	4,400
Newport – Platform Loco Tkts - 2	1,000
Merstone	2,000
Ningwood	1,000
Freshwater	2,000
Medina Wharf	20,000

Next were listed the weighbridges: St Helens - one of 50 tons, Medina Wharf - one of 20 tons

Lister Auto Trucks - Two of these Trucks are used at Ryde Pier Head to haul Luggage Cages between Boats and Trains, and the Trucks which have been used were received at Ryde as under; T1 - 1928, T2 - 1930, T3 & T4 - 1934, T5 & T6 - 1940

There are 100 Luggage Cages in use, the tares of which vary between 7 cwts. and 8 cwts. the Cages Loading Luggage up to 1-ton.

ROLLING STOCK

Bogie Coaches			Wagon Stock	
LBSCR	60		Open Goods	449
LC & D	39		Covered Vans	51
IWC	1		Rail & Timber Single Bolsters	20
			Highway Vehicle Flats	15
4 Wheeled Coaches				
LC & D	3		Service Vehicles	
			2 Ton Crane	1
Bogie Guards Vans			5 Ton Crane	1
LSW	9		10 Ton Crane	1
LC & D	2		Match Trucks	2
			Tool Vans	4
4 Wheeled Guards Vans			Boiler Truck	1
LSW	1		Tank Truck	1
LC & D	1		Weed Killing Tanks	2
			Weed Killing Brake Van	1
4 Wheeled Horse Box			Tar tanks	2
LBSCR	1		Cattle Wagons	3
			Ballast Wagons	20
4 Wheeled Open Carriage Truck	1		CME & Loco	12
			Goods Brakes	13
Ryde Pier Tramway				
Drewry Petrol Cars	2			
Trailer Cars	2			
Luggage Trailer	1			
Total Vehicles	123		Total Vehicles	559

Opposite page -

I.W.C. 4-4-0T No.6 stands against the familiar background of Newport loco sheds, with feint signs of I. W. C. lettering on the tank sides.
Compared to P.54 she has lost her side chains and the footplate toolbox and the feed pipes to the clack valve have been rearranged to make room for the Westinghouse air pump.
Interestingly, according to Bradley, she was supposed to be Westinghouse fitted by Black, Hawthorn before delivery. Two photos dated to 1890 (including that on P.54) show no sign of a pump in the usual places, so was it fitted between the frames, as in certain modern cases, or was it fitted after arrival?

Number of Set Trains – 20
Ryde Based:

Set No	Coach	Description	Compartments	Seats 1st	Seats 3rd	Weight Tons
489 R	4155	3rd Brk. C.	6		60	24
	4156	3rd Brk C	6		60	24
	6362	Compo C	7	24	40	21
	6363	Compo C	7	24	40	23
	2410	3rd	8		80	21
	2411	3rd	8		80	21
490 R	4170	3rd Brk. C.	4		40	25
	4173	3rd Brk C	7		70	26
	2423 ‖	3rd E	8		80	21
	6344	Compo C	8	24	50	26
	6394 *	Compo E	7	24	40	21
491 R	4171	3rd Brk. C.	4		40	25
	4174	3rd Brk C	7		70	26
	6345	Compo C	8	24	50	26
	6395 *	Compo E	7	24	40	21
	2422 ‖	3rd E	8		80	21
492 R	4172	3rd Brk. C.	4		40	24
	4175	3rd Brk C	7		70	26
	6346	Compo C	8	24	50	26
	6396 *	Compo E	7	24	40	21
	2421 ‖	3rd E	8		80	21
493 R	4109 *	3rd Bke W	5		50	20
	4117	3rd Bke E	7		70	21
	2427 ‖	3rd E	8		80	21
	2428 ‖	3rd E	8		80	21
	6359	Compo E	6	24	30	19
	6397 *	Compo E	7	24	40	21
494 R	4161	3rd Bke C	7		70	24
	2430	3rd E	8		80	21
	2431	3rd E	8		80	21
	2436	3rd E	7		70	20
497 R	4141 *	3rd Bke W	7		70	23
	2418	3rd E	7		70	19
	2419	3rd E	7		70	19
	2420	3rd E	7		70	19
	6358	Compo E	6	24	30	19
	6385 ‖	Compo W	7	24	40	21

AUDIT TIME ON THE ISLE OF WIGHT

Set No	Coach	Description	Compartments	Seats 1st	Seats 3rd	Weight Tons
500 R	4162	3rd Bke C	6		60	24
	2407	3rd C	9		90	24
	6348	Compo C	8	24	50	26
	6349	Compo C	8	24	50	26
	1012	Gds Van E				19
502 R	4168	3rd Bke C	5		50	25
Bembridge	2437	3rd E	7		70	20
Bch	6347	Compo C	8	24	50	26
Loose R	2404 (490)	3rd C	9		90	26
(Set Number	2405 (491)	3rd C	9		90	25
In brackets)	2406 (500)	3rd C	9		90	24
	2412 (492)	3rd C	9		90	20
	2413	3rd C	9		90	21
	2429	3rd E	8		80	21
Guards Vans	1003	4 Whld W				12
	1008	4 Whld E				11
	1014	Bogie W				19
	1015	Bogie W				19
	1020	Bogie W				19
	1021	Bogie W				19
	1022	Bogie W				19
	1023	Bogie W				19
Mail	4124	3rd Bke 4 Whld E	2			11
	4133	3rd Bke 4 Whld	2			11

Newport Based:

Set No	Coach	Description	Compartments	Seats 1st	Seats 3rd	Weight Tons
485 N	4151	3rd Bke C	6		60	24
	4157	3rd Bke C	7		70	26
	6353	Compo C	8	24	50	26
486 N	4152	3rd Bke C	6		60	24
	4158	3rd Bke C	7		70	26
	6354	Compo C	8	24	50	26
487 N	4153	3rd Bke C	6		60	24
	4159	3rd Bke C	7		70	26
	6355	Compo C	8	24	50	26
488 N	4154	3rd Bke C	6		60	24
	4160	3rd Bke C	7		70	26
	6356	Compo C	8	24	50	26

Set No	Coach	Description	Compartments	Seats 1st	Seats 3rd	Weight Tons
495 N	4113	3rd Bke E	5		50	20
	4114	3rd Bke E	5		50	20
	2432	3rd E	7		70	20
	6399	Compo E	7	24	40	21
496 N	4115	3rd Bke E	5		50	20
	4116	3rd Bke E	5		50	20
	2433	3rd E	7		70	20
	6360	Compo E	7	24	40	21
498 N	4118	3rd Bke E	5		50	20
	4121	3rd Bke E	5		50	20
	2434	3rd E	7		70	20
	6388	Compo E	7	24	40	21
499 N	4122	3rd Bke E	5		50	20
	4123	3rd Bke E	5		50	20
	2435	3rd E	7		70	20
	6400	Compo E	7	24	40	21
P & P 503 N	4169	3rd Bke C	7		56	27
Merstone	6367	Compo C	9	19	37	27
Bch	6987	Compo Bke C	7	12	40	27
506 N	4163	3rd Bke C	7		60	24
	4164	3rd Bke C	9		60	24
	6350	Compo C	7	24	50	26
507N	4165	3rd Bke C	7		60	24
	4166	3rd Bke C	9		60	24
	6357	Compo C	7	24	50	26
Loose N	2408 (506)	3rd C	9		90	24
(Set Number	2409 (507)	3rd C	9		90	24
In brackets)	2414 (488)	3rd C	9		90	24
	2415 (485)	3rd C	9		90	24
	2416 (486)	3rd C	9		90	24
	2417 (487)	3rd C	9		90	24
	2424	3rd E	8		80	21
	2425	3rd E	8		80	21
	2426	3rd E	8		80	21
	4103	3rd E	4		46	20
	6986	3rd Bke IWC	4	11	48	26
Mail N	4150	3rd Bke 4 Whld E	2		20	11
Guards Vans N	1017	Bogie W				19
	1018	Bogie W				19
	1019	Bogie W				19
Boat Tk	4381	Converted underframe ex E stock				7½
Horse Bx	3370	4 Whld C	1		5	7

AUDIT TIME ON THE ISLE OF WIGHT

N	Newport Depot	R	Ryde Depot
C	LBSCR	E	LC & D
W	LSWR	*	Dynamo
‖	Wired		

Top - As well as the O2 class the Isle of Wight was synonymous with the graceful Beyer Peacock 2-4-0T designs. Isle of Wight Central No.5 was built for the Ryde & Newport Railway in 1876 and named 'Osborne'. No.5 is shown in the early 1920's at Newport. In spite of keeping the traditional Beyer Peacock outline much has been changed. She has an 1899 replacement boiler, locally cast chimney, steel front bufferbeam, revised cab side sheets and new cylinders fitted in 1903. She was withdrawn as W5 in 1926 after the arrival of more O2 0-4-4Ts.

Lower - Another view of I.W.C. No.6 at Newport, still in as built condition but showing signs of hard work. She carries her original livery with the number in the middle of the tank side surrounded by the company garter. There are no visible signs of a Westinghouse pump, but the front hose shows it was there somewhere!

RYDE PIER TRAMWAY				
Coach No	Description	Seating	Standing	Weight Tons
1	Petrol Car	22	18	4½
2	Petrol Car	22	18	4½
7	Trailer Car	26	22	4
8	Trailer Car	24	24	4
9	Luggage Trailer			1¼

AUDIT TIME ON THE ISLE OF WIGHT

Recorded at Ryde in the same period, were these five views of the Tramway at Ryde. Unfortunately there is no exact date but it is tempting to suggest this was at a time when the Island was still a holiday destination for those wishing to escape from the ravages of an ever increasing wartime country.

The lack of patronage in some of the views, though, is interesting. Were the detail shots deliberately taken to record the scene and exclude people or was it that there was simply no one around? Questions to which we shall never now know the answers. (Any comments however are of course most welcome.)

All photographs from the Howard Butler collection.

The list then continues with details of the number of staff, specifically stated also to be as at the winter of 1940/41.

Traffic Dept		CME Dept	
Ryde Pier Head	31	Newport Works	25
Ryde Esplanade	7	Ryde Works	63
Ryde St John' Road	17	(sub total)	(88)
Brading	10		
St Helens	4	Loco Running Dept	
Bembridge	3	Newport	67
Sandown	8	Ryde	37
Shanklin	7	(sub total)	(104)
Wroxall	3		
Ventnor	9	Engineers Dept.	
Ventnor West	2	Permanent Way	96
Whiwell	1	Building Dept	45
Ashy	1	Lighting	2
Haven Street	2	Water	2
Wootton	3	Outdoor Machinery	2
Whippingham	2	Signalling and Telegraph	6
Newport	43	(sub total)	(153)
Alverstone	2		
Newchurch	2	Grand total	578
Horringford	2		
Merstone	3		
Blackwater	2		
Shide	3		
Medina Wharf	31		
Mill Hill	4		
Cowes	7		
Ningwood	3		
Yarmouth	5		
Freshwater	4		
Newport A D S O	12		
(sub total)	(233)		

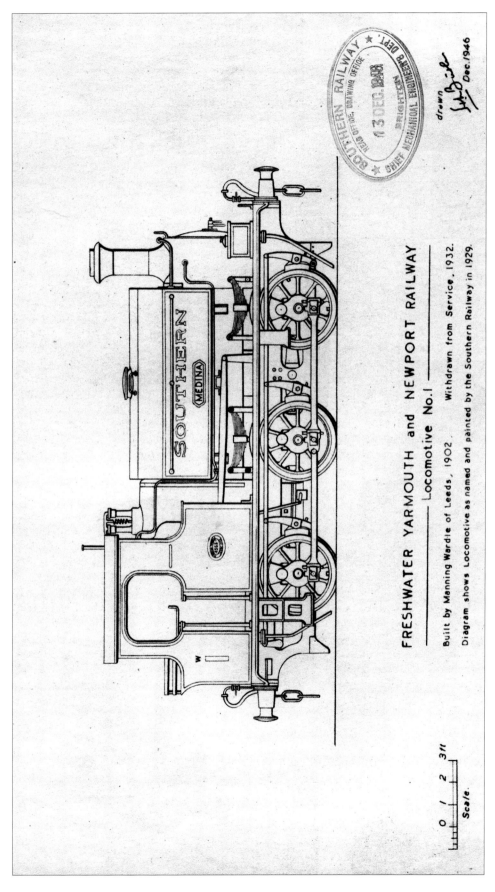

FRESHWATER YARMOUTH and NEWPORT RAILWAY

Locomotive No.1

Built by Manning Wardle of Leeds, 1902.   Withdrawn from Service, 1932.

Diagram shows Locomotive as named and painted by the Southern Railway in 1929.

Scale.   0 1 2 3ft

Manning Wardell 'Q' class saddle tank, purchased by the FYN second hand on 4th June 1913 from civil engineering contractors Pauling & Elliott for £725. With its former owners it had been No 56 and borne the name 'Northolt'. Dating from February 1902 the engine was used on at least two mainland railway contracts, Northolt Junction to High Wycombe, and Limpley Stoke to Camerton. Under independent FYN ownership livery was emerald green with black bands and white lining, the saddle tank lettered 'FYN'. Under the Southern it was painted Maunsell green in May 1924 and named as seen in late 1928, the loco continued to work what was by now its regular duty, shunting Medina Wharf, until laid aside in June 1932. The reason for this was because it was replaced by an 'E1' tank. A year later it was returned to Eastleigh for breaking up and which, according to Bradley, took place in 1933. Having therefore not been in stock since 1932, it is perhaps all the more surprising to find this drawing dated some years later and complete with official SR stamp, is Bradley then correct, or did it even see some further use when returned to the mainland? The date of the drawing raises the questions Possibly a simple exercise in nostalgia or an exercise for a Drawing Office student.

65

Following on are details of the methods of signalling in use on the various lines; again this is information already reproduced elsewhere. Likewise details of level crossings and whether they are operated by residential crossing staff or station staff. Details of tunnels and gradients are provided and the list concludes with information on Medina Wharf:

Lift of Transporter Grab from ground: 27 feet
Swing of Grab from Boat to back of Quay: 120 feet.

Capacity of Grab		No of Lifts / Hour
Steam Coal	30	30 – 50
Gas Coal	25	30 – 50
Sugar Beet	20	30 - 50

Capacity of Coal Depots: 15-16,000 tons.

Having compiled the information the next question is why? Four possibilities come to mind. The first is this was a simple logistical exercise, as may well have been carried out elsewhere from time to time, the fact that no similar record has so far been uncovered for elsewhere is pure coincidence and certainly does not mean they do not exist. Possibly this would be the type of endeavour that would be compiled by a trainee as part of gaining experience.

Next is a similar option, and related to the possibility that Waterloo may not have even known what equipment it actually had on the Island!

Before discussing the third option we should perhaps consider the previous two. At the time 1940/41 it is unlikely there would have been spare staff available to compile as thorough a list as this. Already the Southern Railway were being stretched in consequence of air raid damage as well as the need for numerous special trains, required for military and government purposes. Possibly the additional services aspect was not so likely on the Isle of Wight, but staff would still be undertaking air raid precautions work and accordingly the duties they would be performing would have increased.

The second option, Waterloo not being aware of the resources and facilities on the Island, is perhaps slightly closer to a possible true reason. The District Office at Newport would no doubt have had details of Traffic Department personnel and resources, but this was just one department and possibly their own records may not have been so up to date.

In the opinion, then, of the present writer the listing may well have been compiled as a means of recording the railway facilities in the event of a German invasion. Bear in mind the Channel Islands had come under German occupation in July 1940 and there was afterwards a genuine fear that the Isle of Wight could well be next, being seen and as the ideal springboard for a full blown landing onto the mainland. (There was a number of 'false alarms' over an invasion of the Island around this time.) By having such a record, albeit still lacking in some obvious detail – spare stocks of essential equipment, rails, sleepers, here was a means for the SR to know what they might need to run a normal service following a restoration to peace at some stage in the future. Possibly even at the time of compilation a specific threat existed and the papers represented all the information it was possible to assimilate within a limited time, maybe even drawing together the records of the respective departments into one place. Against this is the fact that the document is not marked as 'Restricted' or 'Secret'. No doubt the historical aspects could well have been included later.

The forth option is the easiest still. The record was the work of an enthusiast supportive of the Island railways. Possibly a railwayman, even a local railwayman.

Whatever and why ever, the final question we cannot answer is that of the authorship, for no names are mentioned. The papers were located in the records of the late Hermann Butler, a Southern Railway member of staff who had completed his pupilage at Eastleigh in the mid 1930s, and a native Englishman also, despite the name.

We know Hermann spent some time working at Ryde around 1942 – as witness the accompanying photographs taken around that time, so was this even something he brought back with him, or was it even he who compiled it earlier?

Research of any type can be both fascinating and rewarding although, in a situation such as this, new information reveals questions that cannot in all probability nowadays ever be fully answered. Even so it remains a fascinating record as well as a perplexing enigma.

I would like to thank Howard and Linda Butler for their assistance in the compilation of these notes. Also to Dave Hammersley for advice with the captions.

...and finally on the Island,

A MYSTERY LOCO

by Dave Hammersley

This sad little scene turned up, tucked into the back pocket of a pre-WW2 photo album. With no notes on the print some detective work was needed. It was immediately obvious that it was a Terrier, with its circular buffer back plate bigger than the bufferbeam itself. The question was, which one?

The non-standard reinforcing plate round the coupling pocket threw me for a moment, but eventually confirmed the locos identity. Most of you will have noticed, before me, the No.9 on the bufferbeam!

What we see though is a Stroudley A1 class Terrier, Southern Railway number W9, not to be confused with the later W9 'Fishbourne', which was an A1X. She is being broken up in the sidings at St Helens in 1927. The site is also probably very close to where she came ashore on delivery to the Isle of Wight.

How she came to be here is a sad story as it appears she was working a Bembridge branch train when a complete failure of the crank axle occurred. Consequently she was not deemed fit either for removal to Ryde, nor for repair and was cut up at the nearest convenient point.

No 9 was one of the first batch of Terriers, built at Brighton in late 1872 as No.72 'Blackwall'. After service in London and around Brighton she was purchased in 1899 by the Isle of Wight Central Railway under an early form of hire purchase. In 1917 she received a second hand A1 boiler and a new, locally cast chimney. At about the same time the bunker was extended to the rear bufferbeam in a style which became characteristic of all the Island Terriers.

With the formation of the Southern she was repainted into Maunsell livery as W9, but time was running out. She was condemned in April 1927 and moved to St Helens on the Bembridge branch where she was broken up. This is where we see her surrounded by bits of her own boiler, tanks and cab.

The sidings at St Helens were frequently used for scrapping and there seems to be a continuous line of debris to the right. A lot of early Isle of Wight Central coaches were scrapped at about this time and it is probably the remains of these that we can see. The open wagon next to No.9 already contains some wheelsets and it could be that these have been removed from No.9 for reuse on other Terriers. There is no sign of wheels protruding through the footplate.

Real Atmosphere

Some photographs need no explanation, with others, perhaps, a comment from the photographer is enough. Indeed I recall being told years ago that if a long caption is required then that is defeating the object. Whatsoever school you may hail from I hope you will appreciate what can only be described as the photographers art seen here.

In some ways views such as these might also be seen as tribute to the end of Southern Steam, although as the present text is likely to be read in Spring 2008 at the earliest, it can hardly be said to be suitable as an anniversary commemoration for what had taken place in July 1967.

On the left, the scene is St George's Hill cutting, between Walton on Thames and Weybridge in May 1967. The scene once commonplace, but rarely recorded. What would today's Health & Safety say about a hundredweight of signal arm crashing down to the horizontal a few inches from the men?

Above is the end of Platforms 14 / 16 at Waterloo in November 1966. The unit is probably a 4-COR bound for Portsmouth, the steam locomotive needs no explanation.

No prizes for guessing who the photographer, Rod Hoyle of course.

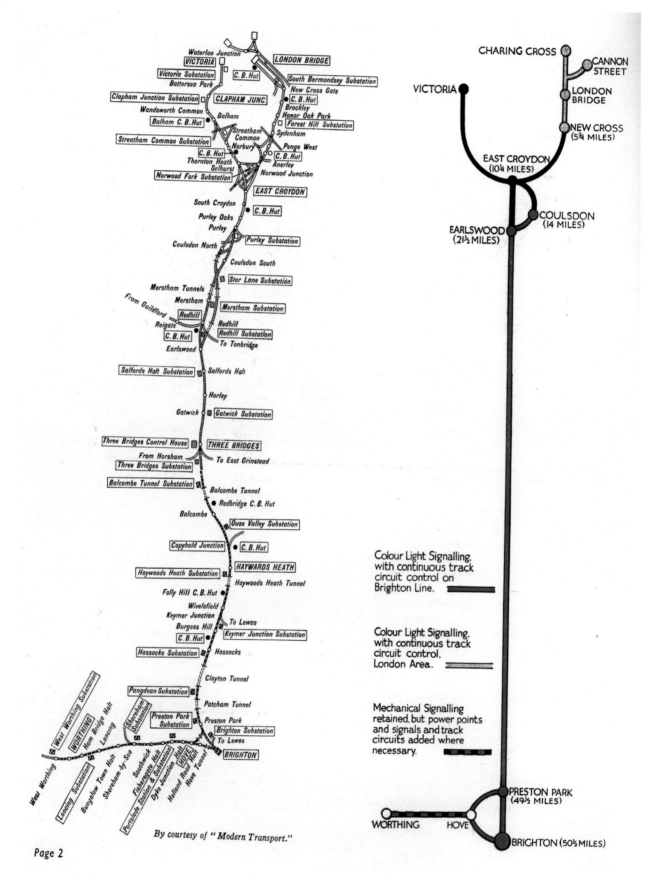

By courtesy of "Modern Transport."

Page 2

The 1932
BRIGHTON LINE RESIGNALLING
Part 1

First announced by the Southern Railway in 1930, the resignalling of the Brighton Line by the Southern Railway in 1932 was just one part of the £2.7 million major upgrading of the line together with the associated electrification to Brighton and Worthing approved by the SR on 10th October 1929.

Most of the funding for the upgrading, electrification and signalling works between Coulsdon North, Brighton and Worthing came from the Southern Railway's share of the 'Railway Passenger Duty' levy, which was abolished in the 1929 budget. The capitalised value of which was to be spent on schemes to relieve unemployment.

At the time the estimated cost of the signalling work was put at £162,000 and to incorporate colour light signalling, as a means to "…reduce considerably the delays caused to services by adverse punctuality particularly in foggy weather."

The work commenced in 1931 and was contracted by the Southern Railway to the Westinghouse Brake & Signal Company Ltd – formerly the Westinghouse Brake & Saxby Signal Company Ltd, who had most recently been involved in signal modernisation on the SR between London Bridge and New Cross in 1929.

With the new electric services scheduled to start at the end of 1932, it was essential that all the new and modified signalling installations were completed prior to their introduction. Whilst a considerable amount of factual information relative to the new work has survived, we do not have dates for the commencement of work on the various sections of the line.

Personnel from both Westinghouse and the Southern Railway were involved with the prior testing of the installations. Joint commissioning teams being used to effect the actual changeover from old to new.

All the new work was brought into use in stages, the first section between Coulsdon North and immediately north of Balcombe Tunnel being introduced on Sunday 5th June 1932 and was completed in just six hours. During that time the following signal boxes were taken out of use:

Cane Hill
Quarry
Worsted Green
Earlswood Station
Tinsley Green
Three Bridges North
Three Bridges South

The former central box at Three Bridges now controlled the whole area of the station with remote operation of turnouts previously worked from the North and South cabins, although some turnouts in the immediate vicinity of the central box remained manually operated. The installation of the new work at Three Bridges was made all the more difficult by having to install the replacement lever frame in the same cabin as the old one and while it was still in use, so reducing the space the signalmen had available to work the traffic.

Other signal boxes at Star Lane, Horley North, Horley South, and Gatwick Racecourse (later Airport) were retained, but only opened as required, such as for ballast trains, goods workings, and race specials; otherwise they were switched out of circuit. However,

Upper-quadrant semaphore signals, with 2-aspect colour-light distants - Earlswood Junction. (See comment on Page 76.)

Three Bridges signal box during the installation of the new locking frame - seen on the right. A view of the interior of Keymer Crossing featured on Page 32 of Issue No 2 of 'The Southern Way'.

(Unless stated otherwise all illustrations accompanying this article are from 'The Railway Gazette'.)

unlike a mechanical block worked installation, where having a signal box switched out of circuit meant an increase in the length of the block section and a consequential reduction in line capacity. In this case, as the whole route was track circuited, a feature of the installation was that it was possible to switch the main running signals into automatic operation.

A week later on Sunday 12th June changes were made at Copyhold Junction, just over a mile north of Haywards Heath and where, previously, the Ardingly lines which had run parallel with the Brighton main line as a separate pair of tracks, diverged. Instead the new arrangements saw the outermost tracks designated as up and down local lines and the centre pair as up and down through lines, which also had their direction of running changed. This work was arranged to coincide with the introduction of the new signal box at Haywards Heath which replaced the former North and South cabins as well taking the place of Copyhold Junction signal box, the physical junction now remotely controlled from Haywards Heath.

The new signal box at Haywards Heath, aside from the one at Brighton, was the only totally new construction, it had a Westinghouse 'A2' frame of 60 levers and also controlled 11 remote turnouts by electrical means together with associated colour light signals. In this way the layout at Copyhold Junction was brought under the direct control of Haywards Heath. Emergency operation of remote turnouts was possible by removing individual handles from separate point controllers located within the locking area of the frame. Where more than one remote turnout was controlled from a particular box, the handles were similarly unique and there was no chance of confusion leading to illegitimate hand-operation of a machine in an emergency or during maintenance duties.

Following the commissioning of Haywards Heath, the new automatic signals between Balcombe Tunnel and Haywards Heath were brought into use on Monday 3rd October, the changeover taking just 15 minutes for each line. The final section of automatic signalling southwards from Haywards Heath to the north end of Preston Park came into use on Thursday 6th October, this time taking the engineers one hour to carry out the work.

Colour light signals were used throughout the running lines which were physically similar to many still seen in operation today. These included many automatic signals – the aspect displayed being governed by the occupation of the track circuit ahead of the signal, which when clear allowed the signal to display a yellow aspect, the green aspect was displayed when the next signal ahead was showing a proceed aspect, many automatic signals spent much of their life displaying a green aspect. Where an automatic signal was located to the rear of a semi-automatic or controlled signal then the automatic signal would normally display a yellow aspect, the normal aspect of the signal ahead being red. If the signal ahead was a semi automatic that was in automatic mode and displaying a proceed aspect then the aspect would be green.

Semi automatic signals operated as controlled signals when the controlling signal box was open and as automatic signals when it was switched out. Additionally, as an indication to drivers, the letter 'A' was displayed electrically on the semi-automatic signals whenever the controlling box was out of circuit – switched out. This indication was obtained after all of the controlling signal levers had been reversed in the signal box after which the 'King' lever (one for each road) was similarly reversed to complete the process of switching the box out of circuit.

The display of the letter A for 'automatic' – was only seen when the red aspect was shown. This was also an indication to a driver brought to a stand at such a signal that he may, after waiting three minutes for the signal to clear, proceed cautiously past the red aspect as far as the line is clear or until he reached the next signal.

Not surprisingly this proviso was rigidly described in the 'yellow' notices as under, this example from Signalling Instruction No 23 of 1932, together with parts of No 40 of 1932.

'PASSING RUNNING SIGNALS AT DANGER'

(Extracts from Regulation 25B of the Train Signalling Regulations between Stone Hall and Folly Hill boxes.)

(a) Automatic signals will exhibit an illuminated letter 'A' when at danger. The exhibit of the letter 'A' is an indication to Drivers and Guards that the 'Wait and proceed' arrangement is authorised at such signals.

(b) A Driver on stopping at a signal in obedience to the danger aspect, must, if the aspect of the signal does not change in the interval and PROVIDED THE SIGNAL EXHIBITS AN ILLUMINATED LETTER 'A', 'wait' thereat three minutes, give one long whistle and then 'proceed' cautiously at a speed not exceeding 5 MILES AN HOUR as far as the line is clear or as far as the next signal, being prepared to stop clear of any obstruction.

"In the event of a signal (which is exhibiting an illuminated letter 'A') being passed at danger and the next signal when appearing in sight is found to be showing a green, two yellow or one yellow aspect, the Driver must not assume that it has been operated for his train to proceed but must satisfy himself by personal observation that the whole of the section up to that signal and to a point about ¼ mile ahead of such signal is clear of obstruction, and he must continue to proceed cautiously as far as the line is clear or to the next signal beyond.

"In the event of a Driver passing a signal at danger under the 'wait and proceed' arrangement, and he has reason to believe that the detention is due to a failure, and not to the occupation of the line ahead by another train, he must report accordingly at the next station or signal box open (stopping especially if necessary), giving full particulars of the number of the signal concerned. Similar action must be taken if irregular aspects are exhibited or if a Driver has any other reason to suspect that a failure has occurred.

"(c) When a train is brought to a stand at a running signal, which is at Danger and which is not exhibiting an ILLUMINATED letter 'A', the Driver must, if a Hand Signalman is not provided at the signal and if the signal aspect is not changed in the interval, wait three minutes and then proceed to the telephone, if available at the spot and obtain instructions from the Signalman. In communicating with the Signalman the Driver must be careful to state, clearly, at which signal the train is detained and not proceed until the signal aspect is changed or he is authorised to pass the signal.

"In the event of a failure of the signal, the Signalman or the Hand Signalman, as the case may be, must inform the Driver accordingly and, provided the section of the signal concerned is clear, authorise the Driver to pass the signal. In such circumstances the Driver must give one long whistle and proceed cautiously towards the

Automatic signals between Three Bridges and Gatwick. In the background are Apparatus Cases containing Relays, Track feed sets etc.

Up Home Signals, Copyhold Junction. The height to the centre of the red lens of the running signals varied between 10½ and 17½ feet from rial level. The actual bulbs used being 12v, 25 watt 3-pin bulbs. Separate sidelights were also fitted where appropriate to enable motormen to draw up very close to a signal. These side lights quickly became known as 'pigs-ears'. Back lights were not provided.

next signal, being prepared to bring his train to a stand immediately should the occasion require. If the signal is at danger owing to a track circuit failure the provisions of Regulation 25A must be observed.

"(d) Should the light of a signal be out, the Driver must, if a Hand Signalman is not provided at the signal, stop and immediately proceed to the telephone, if available, at the spot, and obtain instructions from the Signalman In communicating with the Signalman the Driver must be careful to state clearly at which signal the train is detained and that the light of the signal is out.

In the event of the main light of a running signal being out but the side light is showing an aspect other than red, Drivers must first bring their trains to a stand and then proceed cautiously, being prepared to stop at the next signal if necessary. The circumstance must be reported to the next station - or signal box open (stopping especially if necessary).

"(e) Should a Driver, when using the telephone at a signal in accordance with clauses (c) and (d), be unable to communicate with the Signalman owing to a failure of the instrument, or should a telephone not be available at the spot where the train has stopped, the Fireman, or Motorman of an electric train, must go to the signal box for instructions.

(f) In the event of circumstances arising in connection with an electric train, which necessitate the Guard riding in the leading cab, as provided in Instruction 60 (a) of the Instructions Applicable to the Electrified Lines (Direct Current Conductor Rail System), dated 8th June, 1925, the Guard will be held responsible for carrying out the duties of the Driver as laid down in the foregoing instructions."

Controlled signals displayed an aspect which was dependent upon the condition of the relevant track circuits and any point detection in the route. With two exceptions all the running signals were of the 3-aspect 'Red-Yellow-Green', the exceptions being some four aspect signals on the approach to Preston Park and either side of Patcham Tunnel. (Four aspect colour lights signals of both the vertical and cluster type had first been used, not only on the Southern Railway but for the first time in the world, in the resignalling of the section between Holborn Viaduct and Elephant & Castle, which was brought in to use on 21st March 1926).

A modern, but not totally new feature for the period was to designate the signals and associated controlling boxes with a pair of letters - and the relevant number in the case of the actual signals. The prefix 'C' was reserved for the 'Central Section' with the Brighton line boxes prefixed as follows:

Brighton	CB
Preston Park	CC
Clayton Cutting	CD
Hassocks	CE
Burgess Hill	CF
Keymer Crossing	CG
Haywards Heath	CH
Balcombe Station	CJ
Balcome Tunnel	CK
Three Bridges	CL
Gatwick Racecourse	CM
Horley South	CN
Horley North	CP
Salfords (local lines only)	CQ
Earlswood	CR
Star Lane	CS
Coulsdon No 2	CT

Of these, Star Lane, Salfords, Horley North, Horley South, Gatwick Racecourse, Balcombe Station, Burgess Hill, Hassocks, and Clayton Cutting only opened 'as required'.

Automatic signals – regardless of the location were designated CA followed by the allocated signal number. These letters and numbers were displayed on a plate carried on the signal post – again akin to present day practice.

With the exception of Brighton, where a Westinghouse Style `L' power frame was provided, all the other signalling alterations were based on the use of adapted mechanical lever frames, Three Bridges Central receiving a new lever frame and Haywards Heath a new signal box and Westinghouse A2 frame. Elsewhere the existing frames were adapted for their new role by the fitting of locks and controllers to work the electrical circuits and colour light signals. Most of the existing shunt signals and points continued to be worked mechanically, albeit mostly with electrical detection.

The distinction between boxes to be closed and those being retained was based on those from which routing of trains was carried out; where shunting takes place, or where special regulation of traffic may occasionally be necessary. The one odd exception was Keymer Junction, where the nearby Keymer Level Crossing box was retained to work the level crossing, control of the junction being transferred to the crossing box and the junction box abolished. (The changeover of control of the junction points, from the Junction signal box to the Crossing signal box was accomplished in just 17 minutes.)

Two signals were located within Clayton Tunnel (2,266 yards) – one on each of the up and down lines. These were classed as 'repeaters' with each having the ability to display only a yellow or green aspect. There was then no danger of a train being brought to rest within the actual tunnel. although the disadvantage was that this made a for a very long section between signals – in excess of 2,600 yards, thus reducing the potential for line occupancy.

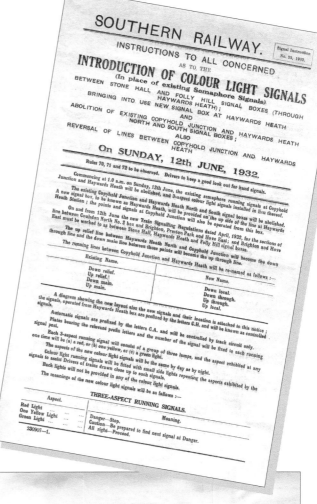

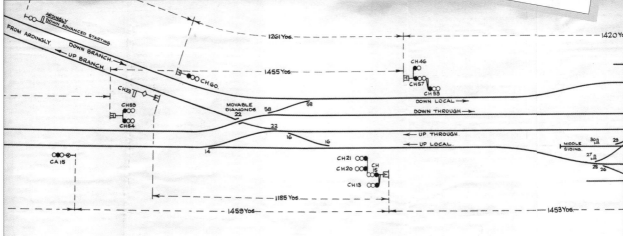

Extract example from 'Yellow Notice' (Signal Instruction No 23, 1932), the part plan seen depicting Copyhold Junction.
Colin Hall collection.

Above - *Part of the subway under the running lines at Brighton Station, at the time being used for mechanical connections but later for signal cables under the new installation.*

Some semaphore signals, in rear of the first colour light signal of the new installations, were provided with approach lights. An example was the up branch inner home at Keymer Crossing – CG15 on the diagram. This consisted of a two aspect colour light signal head placed under the stop arm on a semaphore post, and would only display the appropriate yellow or green aspect if the semaphore arm were in the 'off' position. (Over thirty years later a similar approach-light arrangement was provided for the down branch home signal at Winchester Junction controlling the exit off the Mid Hants line, whilst in 2007, a similar provision still exists on the up line outside Bognor Regis signal box.)

The introduction of the new signalling south of Balcombe Tunnel allowed for further economy in the number of boxes and eight signal boxes were closed:

Balcombe Intermediate
Stone Hall
Folly Hill
Copyhold Junction

Above - *The interior of the new Brighton box and very much a showpiece at the time. Indeed, Sir Herbert Walker referred to the installation here as , "...a marvel of the engineering world." Aside from the works mentioned elsewhere in this article, it was not surprising that the modernisation featured heavily in several contemporary journals, including 'The Railway Gazette' and 'Southern Railway Magazine'. Some years later, in 1948, John Webb recounted having worked here as a booking boy. "There were three signalman in the box all the time, the men looking after Main and East being the senior, the junior man being on the West. Having said that, some men would prefer to stay where they were and consequently three men worked just the West side, whilst six rotated around Main and East. It was a good job although discipline was very strict."*

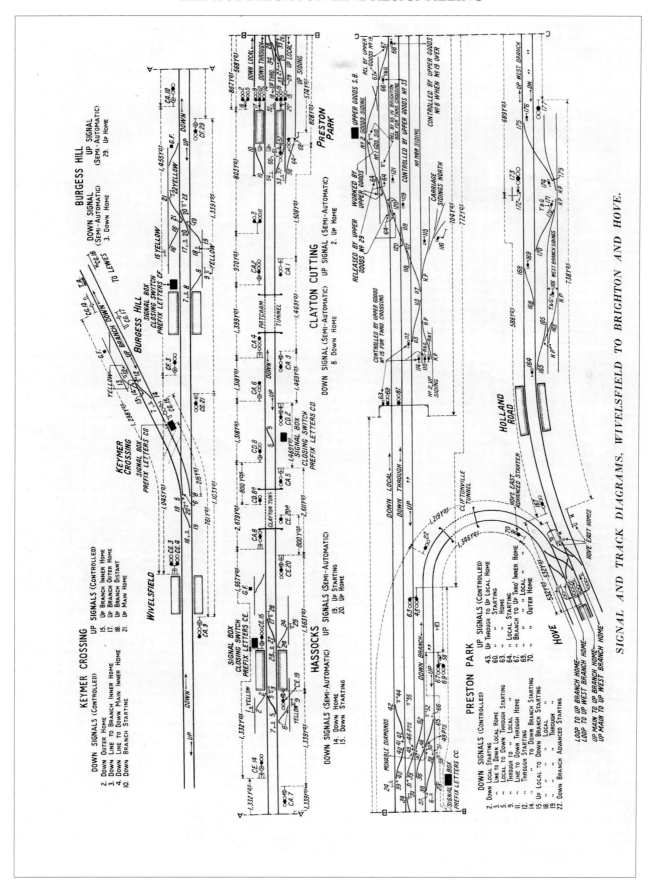

SIGNAL AND TRACK DIAGRAMS, WIVELSFIELD TO BRIGHTON AND HOVE.

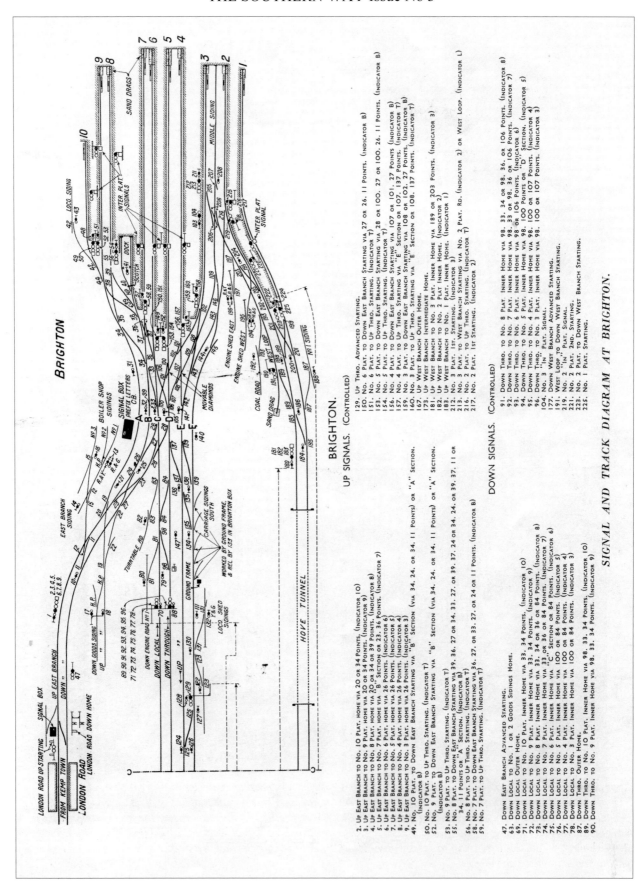

SIGNAL AND TRACK DIAGRAM AT BRIGHTON.

Wivelsfield Station
Keymer Junction
Brapool Cutting
Patcham

With the exception of Keymer Junction, all of these were boxes which either could or would have spent long periods switched out of circuit.

On Sunday October 16th 1932 the new signalling was brought into use at Preston Park and Brighton in just 6½ hours commencing at 12.05 am. Nor were the train services affected, but continued to operate, albeit of course at what was a restricted frequency, during the small hours.

At Preston Park the work involved the closure of the former Preston Park North Box with all signalling now controlled from the former South cabin. As at Haywards Heath, remote operation of turnouts formerly under local control was introduced and operated by Westinghouse point motors.

Approach control was applied to Preston Park Down Home signal for trains routed into the down loop (platform road). This meant that a train destined for the loop would have to pass signal CA2 at yellow, which would then have to return to red before the following signal, Preston Park No 3 could change from its normal red indication, to one of a single yellow. In this way the necessary reduction of speed, to take the turnout safely, was achieved. One variation that will be noted, however, when comparing 'like for like', was the physical appearance of the various colour light signals, particularly where two or more routes were available. At that time separate signal heads were provided for each route and when cleared would indicate a full aspect sequence for the appropriate route. This of course was exactly as per semaphore practice. It would be some time before the Southern Railway employed a single signal head, accompanied by a junction indicator (feathers) for this purpose.

The concluding part of this article will appear in Issue No 4 in September 2008.

Spot the wagon…. *One of the items that seems to create the most interest amongst enthusiasts is that related to Private Owner wagons. The excellent series of books by Lightmoor Press on this topic as well as the sought after earlier volumes by Bill Hudson all bear witness to the fact. We are pleased, then, to present the first of a number of views featuring PO Wagons which we intend to use. The location here is Banstead, on 23rd April 1935 with E3 No 2169 shunting. Vehicles belonging to Messrs Beattie, POP, Thorne, and Bartlett are visible as well, of course, as various common user vehicles.* H F Wheeler / R S Carpenter

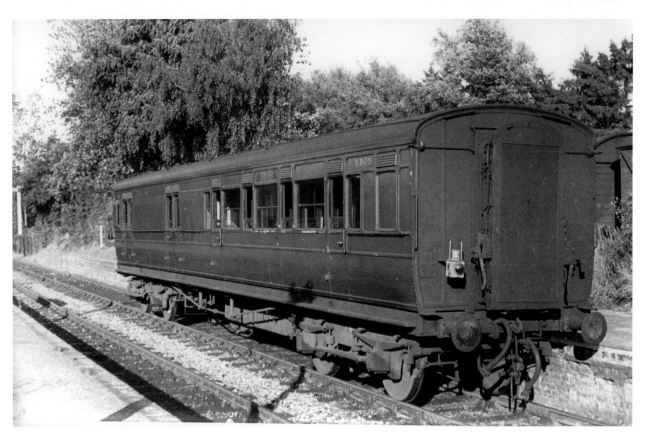

Opposite page, top - The Southern did not operate many single coach trains, two-coach sets being the norm for branch line and lightly loaded services. In fact it had a relatively small number of coaches specifically allocated to branch lines, where the loading was exceptionally light and there was little daily fluctuation in loading. In photograph 1 we see a Kent & East Sussex line train from Headcorn to Tenterden at High Halden Road on 13th August 1952 formed of Ol class loco No 31065, ex SECR five- compartment Brake 3rd S 3291 and a van. A regular performer on the KESR at this period, S3291 (original SECR number 860) was one of 20 similar coaches to Diagram 147 with a body length of 50 ft 1 in. The first 15 were built by the SECR and the last five, including 3291, by the Metropolitan Railway Carriage and Wagon Company. It would appear to be still in Southern Railway green but with an S prefix to the number and BT (Brake Third) stenciled at the extreme lower right hand end of the body. By the early fifties many of these vehicles had gone into departmental use; however, the last two survived in revenue service until early 1958.

Opposite page, lower - On the same day ex LSWR Corridor Brake Third S 3175 waits at Tenterden station KESR for its next working on the western section of the line to Robertsbridge. 3175, again probably still in SR green, was one of 20 57ft Brake Thirds built in 1921 to LSWR Diagram 3151 as LSWR no 1337. These were the last LSWR vehicles to be built in the traditional panelled style. Comprising 4 compartments (seating 32), a lavatory and a large luggage compartment, it is clear that rather more traffic was expected in parcels and miscellaneous goods than in passengers! Several coaches of this batch saw service on the line in the late 40s and early 50s, with motive power on the western section of the line usually being an A1X. 3157 was withdrawn in late 1957 and was the last of its type in revenue service. It then survived for a while longer in Departmental use.

Above - Another line where a single coach was operated in the early 50s at off peak times was the Hayling Island branch, again with motive power exclusively from the A1X class of locomotive. This line was especially interesting because of the wide variety of 'odd' stock it seemed to attract and for the intensive service provided at summer weekends. We have already seen the ex SECR steam rail-motor at Hayling Island in Rolling Stock Files No 2. The vehicle shown here, too, has a very interesting history and is almost certainly the vehicle adjacent to the rail-motor. It originated as 48ft Lavatory Bi-composite, built in December 1898 as LSWR no 508 to Diagram 758. Renumbered 2677, it then became SR no 4677 in 1927. The SR included it in their extensive old coach rebuilding programme converting it in April 1936 to 58ft Brake composite no 6404 to Diagram 418, by the addition of a guards van at the near end, complete with LSWR 'ogee' type lookouts and by remounting it on a new 58ft under frame. It was formed into SR two-coach non push-pull set 45 with 58ft Brake third 2639 but was running singly by the late 1940s. It is seen here approaching Langston Bridge bound for Hayling Island behind A1X 32677 on 3rd May 1953 and probably carries BR red livery. Its passenger accommodation comprises two first class compartments four third class and two lavatories. Whether the lavatories were actually required for the 4½ mile, 15 minute journey is debatable! 6404 was withdrawn in December 1956. 32677 was one of the few 'Terriers' which reached the BR era but did not survive into preservation, although its copper caped chimney, seen well here, was transferred to 32655 and is still on that locomotive today at the Bluebell Railway. 3rd May 1953.

'Push-Pull to Alton'

Continuing the popular series of footplate reminiscences from Eastleigh Driver, Hugh Abbinnett.

About a year after my experiences at Southampton Terminus (Southern Way No 1), several things had changed. Firstly, I had now reached the ripe old age of 15 years and 7 months, and I had also gained about a stone in weight. Equally important I had learned to operate a Drummond M7 tank in Push-Pull mode, or to be more accurate perhaps, when 'motor operated' using the compressed air system.

To be fair this was done under the watchful eye of my driver, one Mr George Vivash , who had to satisfy himself that I was capable of not only firing but also driving the engine, as that is, of course, what I would actually be required to do. As those reading this will of course know, the theory was that the driver would operate the train - regulator and brake from the front of the coaching set, although in practice the system even then was a complete failure. Indeed the only advantage was a quicker turnaround at the end of each journey, with perhaps an advantage of 25 minutes which was the average time most stations seemed to take to push back, uncouple, run-around, shunt, recouple, and prepare for the return journey.

By design both the brake and a very unreliable miniature repeating regulator were controlled by the driver, who, try as he might, never achieved the finesse of operation it was possible to obtain on the footplate. Indeed, as the remote control was air operated, there was no gentleness possible and the first movement of the regulator at the coach end was identified by an almost full-blooded rush of steam at the engine end, the steam chest and pistons awash with chalky water. Consequently the train would quickly come to a slow and cumbersome halt; that is until the fireman on the footplate closed the regulator himself and then carefully opened it again although only slightly, which would

succeed in getting the train moving again.

Undaunted, the driver would try again, although after perhaps the third time he had had enough and by the private code of ringing the start and stop button three times, the message was, "...take out the ****** controlling pin...", which meant communication was now on the bells with the brake alone operated by the driver, and the fireman responsible for the regulator and reverser positions.

All this was of course strictly against the rules, although not totally frowned upon as at least it meant the train got to its destination, assuming that the boiler pressure remained high enough, that the coal was of reasonable quality, the water level could be maintained, and everything else remained as it should. Such, then, was what was expected of me on these occasions, "the kid at the back", as all drivers on the push-pull referred to their mates on the footplate.

Of course, before this occurred I had to be officially passed out by the Loco Inspector and consequently one day found me alone on the footplate of the M7 at Eastleigh with said person in authority joining me on the footplate. The test was to watch me perform alone over all of the three miles to the next station at Shawford. But with the fire prepared and the driver up front happy to go along quietly so as to ensure I was able to maintain both steam and water, everything went well.

At Shawford, the next stage was the issue of a formal document proving my competence and to which end the Inspector reached deep into the pocket of his heavy railway Macintosh...although seemingly unable to locate the requisite paperwork. Mumbling "...You'll be alright son," he alighted from the footplate, doffing his trilby in the process, whereupon the necessary form

Opposite top - *The unmistakable public façade of Southampton Terminus, the original station for the town. In many ways more convenient for the centre compared with 'Central, it avoided the long climb up the hill compared with the latter station. Although having been without a train service for over 40 years now, the building survives although nowadays in commercial use. 10th September 1957.* *Leslie Freeman / Transport Treasury 3045*

Opposite lower - *30029 on an Alton push-pull at Eastleigh but seen here in Platform 2, 28th March 1957. The banner repeaters are for the up main line signals and which were located beyond the footbridge and would otherwise be out of sight. They replaced some very tall co-acting arms that could be seen from a far greater distance than was now the case. The lamps lying around was typical of Eastleigh - probably many other locations as well.* *Tony Molyneaux / KJR collection*

was seen to wedged in the greasy headband. A quick signature and he was down the steps ready to cross to the down platform for the trip back to Eastleigh; and all this before we had even started away again.

Aside from the Inspector, the next person to find out about my newly acquired status would be the list clerk at Eastleigh and I might then have been expected to be rostered to the same turn for the next day, and the one after that, and the one after that. But the railway operated in strange ways and despite my newly found qualification, the following day found me back on the more usual freight working, which was more applicable to my age and limited seniority. In theory it was only really senior men in the passed-fireman grade who were supposed to operate the push-pull services. As these men could often be called upon to drive in their own right it was thus useful to have a nucleus of other fireman capable of working these trains. Indeed such was the shortage of firemen at Eastleigh that it was not long before I was rostered to the Alton push-pull workings starting from Southampton Terminus.

Our loco is, of course, an M7, No '128', one of the type with the longer front overhang and two Westinghouse reservoirs. The first of these is under the front framing and the other on top of the right hand side tank. The air pump is similarly fitted on the right hand side of the smokebox. Our duty first involves travelling passenger to Southampton Terminus and collecting our engine, which, when we arrive, had already been prepared and is in the process of being turned on the depot turntable.

We always work the push-pulls with the engine facing towards Southampton, which means the driver is at least looking the right way for the return journey. No '128' is ready to drive off the table as we arrive and so the shed driver leaves us to it - he has a 'Nelson' to attend to which was blowing off noisily as it waits its turn. (So much for the standing instruction that engines should be kept as quiet as possible at the depot, as, like Bournemouth, Eastleigh, and indeed numerous other sheds, the depot was next to a residential area.)

We have to move off the table as quickly as we can and so after just a cursory glance around it is forward to clear the area ready for the 'Nelson'. Immediately the larger engine is moving up to take over our vacated space, a young cleaner perched precariously on the tender breaking up the coal and shovelling it forward ready for the regular fireman.

No 128, though, needed no such attention from me; likewise she has been oiled beforehand and the sandboxes are also full, a useful thing if we encounter a greasy rail on the sharp climb to Medstead from either direction later. The final check is that the smokebox door is secure, after which it is my job to use the telephone to inform the signalman we are ready to depart. He is ready for us as well, as the dummy comes off almost immediately, enabling us to move forward the short distance towards the buffer stops in Platform 2, at which point the station pilot will attach our two coach set.

There are already some passengers waiting for the train as we glide to a halt, where the station pilot, another M7, waits at the north end of Platform 3 ready to cross over and then attach our coaches. At Southampton there is also a passenger shunter, which means the fireman will not have to perform the actual coupling, which is one advantage of push-pull working, meaning one job less when we arrive at Alton.

The two coaches, guided by the shunter waving from the guards' compartment of the set, glide down the platform. The men have clearly done this many times before, as at a predetermined location the set almost comes to rest, at which point the shunter jumps out guiding the pilot engine from the platform over the last few feet. At the same time as calling a halt to the pilot, the shunter is down below the edge of the platform coupling-up. This is followed by the vacuum, heating and air pipes, all far quicker than I could ever manage at that time. The fact there is an engine at both ends of the train also meant that under the rules there is no need to conduct a brake test, although as my driver leaves the footplate, he reminds me he will be testing the communication bell between the driving compartment and the cab.

This I am able to hear ringing out as I change the headlamp to a tail lamp at the smokebox end, acknowledging the ring as I return to the footplate. Then it is just a question of waiting for the signal and the guard, and keeping everything in order, whilst all the time slowly building up steam and water ready for the climb north from Eastleigh, and then on to the steeper but shorter ascent north from Ropley. If everything goes to plan I can then slowly fill the boiler during the lay-over at Alton, but a lot depends on how the engine is behaving, as no two days, even with the same engine, are ever the same.

The signal at the end of the platform now goes to the 'off' position and promptly at 3.40 pm there is the shrill sound of the guard's whistle, which I answer with the engine whistle at the same time as taking off the handbrake. Two rings on the bell from the driver follow, which I acknowledge. The cylinder cocks are opened and as I open the regulator a cloud of wet steam engulfs the front of the engine, temporarily blocking my view ahead. I close the drain cocks before we reach the end of the platform, the little engine barking hard as, with regulator half open and reversing gear well forward, we always aimed for a prompt start. In some ways this is deliberate as no matter how the engine is behaving we always put up a show passing the Terminus loco depot rather than ever admit to difficulties. The same would apply passing Eastleigh and around the station – too many locomen about, so the blower was off, and the crew nonchalantly peering ahead, even if the actual truth might be the water level and steam pressure were hardly where they should be.

As we pass over the level crossing at Chapel, the signalman is exchanging waves with the driver - obviously they know each other, immediately after this comes one ring on the bell, is the indication for me to shut the regulator as we approach our first stop at Northam. Already our two coaches are well filled but a few more passengers squeeze in all the same.

Depending also on how the main line is running we are sometimes held here for a few minutes whilst an out-of-course Bournemouth or London bound train is given priority. Control always seems to think the locals less important, but a delay at the start can mean problems as far as Winchester Junction before we are able to turn off the main line. Another disadvantage of being late is from a personal perspective, as it also means less time for a break at Alton.

Today the signal is thus against us, but not for long and as a Bournemouth service rounds the curve, it seems that almost the moment the last coach disappears from sight, the signal clears and we are off again. Having warmed the cylinders slightly already and having been stopped for less than a minute, I do not bother to open the drain cocks this time, half hoping the first few blasts from the chimney will not be followed by a lessening of the sound and a wheezing from the front end. My gamble proves right and we move off without a problem.

Within a very short time we are slowing again for St Denys, to be met by the porter shouting out 'Alton train' as we arrive, the same call being heard several times over even if some men almost make it appear like 'Halton train' instead. Running into the next station at Swaythling I notice there is no one waiting, indeed no one got off either whilst in the brief time we pause here. I take the opportunity to swing the coal pick at a rather obstructive piece of 'Welsh' blocking the shovelling plate – with only me on the footplate at least there wasn't a need to watch out for the driver's ankles this time!

Approaching Eastleigh I automatically shut off steam and peer out to see which platform we are to be routed into; as expected it is No 1, the Salisbury loop, and as we gently come to rest the doors of the coaches quickly open and it seems we lose half our passengers, who are changing either for the Romsey or Portsmouth lines.

We have 20 minutes to wait at Eastleigh during which time a Southampton Central to Woking stopping passenger train joins us on Platform 2, whilst on the up through line there is often a late running boat train from Millbrook. The latter, although booked to run ahead of us often seems to be late and in consequence will follow us as far as Eastleigh, with the crew exchanging rude gestures with us as they work their way north.

It is also usual for the 'Nelson' on the Woking service at Platform 2 and ourselves to depart exactly at the same time; indeed it almost seems as if the signalman and guards enjoy the inevitable consequence

The author - right, on the footplate of an M7 some years later. Still working for BR at this time, Hugh was one of the former steam men from Eastleigh who volunteered to return to steam in later years. This occasion was at the 1992 Salisbury steam gala.

Left - *Itchen Abbas, 5th October 1957.*
Leslie Freeman / Transport Treasury 3102

Below - *Push pull set No 1, again near to Itchen Abbas, the locomotive was not recorded. Notice the guard is also riding in the front compartment. The set is made up of ex LSWR non-corridor vehicles Nos 2620 and 6488 and was operating in this form between June 1937 and July 1958. (Full details of SR Push-Pull vehicles and sets will of course be found in Mike King's work on the subject.)*
Gerald Daniels

of this happening for whilst a 'Nelson' is certainly easier to get away from a standing start compared with a 'Bulleid', it is still no match with its heavier train compared with our two coaches and we are soon past him with the opportunity again for more gestures. With steam still on, as we pass Allbrook and the north end of the yard complex, we roll slightly on the embankment, the 'Nelson' now some way behind. Now is also the time to ease up slightly, taking in the meadows alongside the River Itchen which runs on the east side of the line and also the hoarding advertising 'You are in the Strong Country', a reference to the ales produced by

Strong's brewery at Romsey.

A glance behind also shows the Woking train starting to catch up and, by easing off, he will catch us up before Shawford where the four line section ends. Whistles are again exchanged and we find ourselves stationary for a couple of minutes, before he clears the section, the points come over and the signal clears allowing us to amble our way past the end of the loop and into Shawford Station. Any crew and indeed the regular passengers can always tell where they are on the approach to Shawford, as there is the phenomena of a length of roaring rails on the up local at this point.

As usual Porter Stratton is on duty at Shawford. I get the bell to start, so blow the whistle briefly, which, on a dry day, will also attract the attention of the inevitable group of children playing on nearby Shawford Downs.

Onwards again and we are heading for Winchester, although on the way the engine sound changes and I notice the Westinghouse air pump has ceased its regular beating and, instead, remains silent except for a wisp of steam emanating from the glands. A mental note is made to attend to this at the next station. The pump is still silent as we roll to a stop at Winchester and as I nip off the engine with a spanner ready for the requisite thump of the machinery. Even though the air control system is not being used, it is better to have the pump visibly working, too many questions could be asked otherwise.

I notice we will probably be collecting a full load of passengers from this point on. The station staff are also quick off the mark here, for they know there will be a Feltham freight following which we need to avoid delaying or else it could well struggle up the gradient and similarly delay other services as well. Consequently it is up to us and, on getting the bell to proceed, it is full back gear (remember the engine is facing towards Southampton), and we accelerate away from the platform leaving a cloud of grey which will deposit itself as cinders on the platforms - something for the porters to sweep up later. The crew on the Winchester shunter, a little 'B4', watch us as we depart in this way although before we have reached the Andover Road bridge I have notched her up a bit and she starts to run sweeter while accelerating at the same time. I now need to repair the damage done to the fire and it comes as a bit of surprise to hear the bell telling me to ease down as George at the front has seen the distant signal for Winchester Junction at caution. I put on the blower to aid combustion, as with the regulator now shut the coal I have just thrown into the box needs to burn through rather than blacken the fire.

Peering ahead the home signal remains obstinately at danger. Ours is the right arm of three on the same bracket, the centre and tallest arm indicating the main line through to Wallers Ash, whilst on the left is the arm which controls the single line down to the 'Western' at Worthy Down. The Alton branch signal will stay at danger until either a down main line working from Wallers Ash has passed, or, as in this case, the single line to Alresford has been cleared by the down working. Sometimes we would pass the down branch train between the junction and Winchester, but this time there has obviously been a delay and as a result the Feltham freight will probably have already been checked behind us.

The wait, though, is not for long and after no more than half a minute another M7 can be both seen and heard accelerating towards us on the down working. As the engine passes us the driver calls something out, possibly he is explaining the delay but with the noise I cannot make it out. Perhaps George hears and will tell me later – that is, of course, if I remember to ask him!

The Winchester Junction signalman is also quick off the mark, as it is only a matter of moments before he has put the tablet back in the machine, 'asked on' for us to Alresford, obtained the tablet again, reversed the road and pulled the starter. George rings the bell and I open the regulator slightly before leaning out to watch him take the tablet from his side window at the front end. George will keep it with him to Alresford. This is better than what happened to some another Eastleigh men a few months earlier…. That particular crew was delighted at having a brand new tank engine to 'run-in' on an Alton freight and on taking the tablet at Winchester Junction, innocently placed it in the toolbox. Unfortunately, this brand new engine had something missing - a bottom to the tool box - and the all important item was deposited on the ballast long before they reached Alresford. The Alresford signalman had to go back on his motorcycle to retrieve it before services could resume.

Two rings on the bell now and we are off towards the first station at Itchen Abbas. The driver would now be keeping a sharp look out for obstructions on the line; foxes and pursuing hounds were probably the most common, although it was not unknown for larger animals, sheep or even cattle, to stray onto the railway.

At Itchen Abbas we come to rest on the down side, opposite the lush green gardens of what was the former up platform, the loop here having been removed long before the time I started on the footplate. As is usual no one gets on and no one gets off although it will be certainly be different at the next stop. From Itchen Abbas we are also now into watercress country and there are several beds visible at intervals on the south side of the line.

With no catch points at either end of the loop at Alresford, Walt, the signalman is only permitted to

The return journey with both men on the footplate. Clearly on this occasion 30029 was not booked to cross any other service at Medstead and Four Marks, as both the home and starting signals are in the off position. The plethora of additional pipes associated with the push-pull system will be noted.

allow one train into the station at a time and as we sometimes cross the pick-up goods here it is a question of who has arrived first as to who is allowed in and who has to wait outside. Consequently steam is shut off as we glide through the cutting and round the left curve towards the station, although we are in luck and the home signal has been cleared, with the goods already simmering quietly in the platform.

Coming to rest the doors open and passengers, mothers with shopping and prams, start to descend. This was the advantage of the train - so much easier for push-chairs and shopping compared with the bus. Indeed even years later when the diesel units had replaced steam, the same easy facilities continued to be provided. We could never have imagined that one day British Railways would manage to close what was such a busy little line and likewise a useful diversionary route.

I take the opportunity to fill the boiler at Alresford, as well as pulling the fire through ready for a round of firing when we leave the station. George would know if I was firing when stationary and his look of disapproval would be enough to stop me. Across on the footplate of the 'Black-motor' on the freight is a young fireman probably on one of his first turns away from the shed. I wonder how he managed on the climb either side of Medstead, especially with a loose coupled train.

Meanwhile on the platform Walt has taken the tablet from the driver and rushed up the stairs – he always seems in a hurry, before the ringing of bells, clanking and crashing of levers and a far more leisurely descent back down the stairs indicates to us that he has exchanged the tablet ready for us to proceed on the next single line section to Medstead and Four Marks.

We, though, are not quite ready to go yet, as there are still some parcels to load. Invariably this will be watercress and the Guard assists if he feels this will help us to keep time. With all safely stowed aboard he swings on his heel with his whistle already in his mouth. A shrill sound, a wave of the flag and the answering wave from George. I am opening the regulator at the same instant as the bell rings, the injector now turned off, rather than run the risk of overfilling the boiler.

Leaving Alresford, we immediately enter what is often a damp cutting, the overhanging trees more than willing to deposit their leaves on the rails during autumn. This is not just a problem that affects us during October either, as the wind would sometimes blow the fallen leaves from the trackside back onto the rails and consequently I play safe and trickle a bit of sand for a distance of perhaps 300 yards. It is time also to add some more coal which needs a few minutes to burn through before we reach Ropley. By that time steam pressure should also slowly be increasing to maximum, ready for the climb beyond the station.

Shortly after passing over the A31 on the outskirts of Bishop Sutton village, I hear George blowing the whistle and looking out see the reason why; three pheasants, two cocks and a hen alongside the track, the males more intent on their 'show' for the benefit of the female, rather than on paying heed to our approach. Sometimes they would fly straight into our path and whilst on a freight we could stop for a moment to gather our prize, passenger workings were more difficult and instead it was tell someone at the next station in the hope that the bird might be waiting for us upon our return.

Ropley with its renowned topiary is next but this time, as the bell rings to start, it is slowly open the regulator to full at same time as gradually letting the lever forward a bit more and the little engine positively barks as she leaves the station and starts the climb. With the increased blast on the fire it is time to add still more coal, although this is also the moment I find a few shovelfuls of slack. With a heavy train and an M7 this might be more of a problem, but the climb is not too difficult today with just two coaches and it is not long before Medstead and Four Marks station will be in sight. Even so, we keep blasting away almost until the front coach reaches the start of the platform, at which point the bell rings, and as I shut the regulator the safety valves immediately lift as the demand for steam has ceased. By opening the firebox doors, though and letting the injector trickle cold water into the boiler the escaping steam quickly ceases and now it will be a question of simply trying to keep the engine quiet, both on the final leg to Alton and likewise at the destination itself.

Despite my efforts, there is no acknowledgement or thanks from the passengers as they alight from the train here and walk past the engine to exit by the gate, save, that is, for one city gent type complete with bowler hat who seems to take great delight in pronouncing that, according to him, we are half a minute down.

I ignore his comment and look forward to the refreshing run down the bank, where a cooling breeze will be most welcome. A whistle from the guard again, a ring on the bell and I open the regulator gently, the

Right - It was some years before the exterior of Alton station lost its evidence of private ownership. Here was the end of the electric service from Waterloo via Farnham after which steam reigned supreme on the three branch lines that once terminated here, the Mid Hants, Meon Valley, and Basingstoke lines.

Sean Bolan

Lower - : *Displaying the characteristic Mid Hants line steam headcode, 30479 awaits departure at Alton for Southampton on 18th April 1952. Clearly the engine has only just run-round its train as the tail lamp can be seen still attached to the rear coach. The vehicles are Maunsell design and were often used on the Mid Hants line either when a non push-pull fitted loco was rostered, as here, or possibly even when a particular working required more accommodation. A similar formation was hastily reinstated in 1957 when there was a sudden shortage of what were then serviceable new diesel units.*

Arthur Tayler

engine just needing to get the train on the move before gravity will take over. Officially we should not exceed 50 mph on the way down, but more than that is quite common, even with a push pull set; that is until approaching Butts Junction, where a clatter of pointwork indicates the junction with Treloars Siding, whilst the Meon Valley route also joins us running parallel on our right. I can tell from the way the vacuum gauge is dropping that George also has the brakes hard on and we are slowing rapidly as we pass the Brewery siding on the left after which Alton station comes into view around the curve.

Arriving at Platform 2 we stop near the footbridge and immediately the train empties. Then it is pull forward slightly as far as the water column, with me stopping the engine this time so as to ensure it is exactly in the right place. With the aid of the driver the tank is refilled, the carriages also serviced by a porter who has the doors open and is busy sweeping any rubbish out onto the platform to be collected shortly.

The final task is to sort out the coal in the bunker and change the lamps, the driver in the meantime topping up the glands and trimmings as well as placing his hand on the various bearings to check their temperature. After this there is time for a break, before building the fire again ready for departure. Later will be a second round trip, not far perhaps geographically, but having to stop and start something like 44 times in total on those two trips takes its toll and I am glad to eventually finish at Southampton before uncoupling and running back light to Eastleigh. "Same tomorrow", shouts George. I acknowledge him, although of course before tomorrow the List Clerk may have other ideas.

Platforms 1 and 2 at Alton. No 3 was on the far side of the Island. Electric services would invariably run into No 1 although on occasions No 3 was also used - 2 was not electrified. With the need to keep steam services from interfering with the electrics, push-pull working directly into platform 2 and avoiding the need to run round was ideal, although passengers had to use the footbridge to exit the station.
Sean Bolan

Right: *Reverting back to an earlier era and prior to electrification. The view is from the Butts Junction end of the site and with just one train visible, a Waterloo to Southampton service running via Alton.*

'REBUILDING' - THE LETTERS AND COMMENTS PAGE

Received just to late for Issue No 2 was this fascinating note from Barry Balderstone concerning the article on the Botley Train Fire as appeared in the 'Preview Issue'.

"At the time of the incident, I was a member of the Southern Carriage & Wagon Society and I gathered C & W notes for contribution to their newsletter.

I would probable have heard about the fire on the day it happened and on Friday 21st September I noticed four burnt-out vans in a siding adjacent to the main Fareham goods yard, near the East signal box. The fifth apparently intact van with them I have noted as an LMS design vehicle M30423M. My notes describe the burnt out bodies as badly distorted and mostly devoid of paint and sporting fresh rust. Remnants of the original painted finish were discernable along the bottom edges and this can be seen in the photograph on Page 90 of the *Preview* Issue.

By 11th October it was possible to see that inscriptions had been applied to the vehicles, M80953, M80907, and M81521. All also carried the words 'No Brake Willesden C & WW'. Another vehicle was similarly lettered E80987 - 'No Brake Stratford MPD.' Interestingly the vehicle numbers and the words 'No Brake' were applied neatly in while paint at roughly the level of the original number transfers. The Willesden and Stratford consignor details below this, in chalk.

By the evening of the 16th the doors had been removed and placed in two 5-plank wagons positioned in the same siding. These wagons were no longer present by the 19th but may have been elsewhere in Fareham yard. By the 22nd the vans themselves had been removed.

With regard to the presence of the LMS BG, could this simply have been conveniently to hand when a vehicle with an operative handbrake was required to secure the cripples in the siding? The actual surviving van from the incident, as it contained Royal Mail, presumably would have been forwarded onto Portsmouth as soon as official formalities had been completed on the day.

I am also curious that the regional 'owners' apparently should have been so keen to reclaim the remains over such long distances. Or were the markings purely for accounting purposes and was the actual destination the C & WW at Eastleigh?"

Information has also been received from Alan Blackburn on the movement of rail from Basingstoke to Woking that featured in Issue 1. It appears the vehicles used for the purpose were underframes from old LSWR and LBSCR coaching stock and whilst the trip seen in the photographs was successful, a following journey from Redbridge saw the whole of the welded rail slip sideways off the vehicles. The resultant chaos can best be imagined. Blame was apportioned to the vehicles and with the result that underframes involved were scrapped.

Finally, thanks as ever to Peter Bailey for reading the text, Dave Hammersley, he of 'Roxey Mouldings' fame and Bruce Murray, photographic genius. *Please do send your comments good or otherwise, they will all be read and responded to.*

'State of the Art' Track Relaying - 1948

Lower - The Track Relaying Machine (often referred to as the TRM) was developed in about 1948, making use of a standard bogie vehicle base for the main lifting machine and an old flat underframe for the air compressor unit, which worked the lifting winches and slewing equipment. The two vehicles were semi permanently coupled, as the compressor hoses between them were not easily separated. The whole unit was propelled by a locomotive to the desired location. This view shows the arms in the working position and the 'bales', which are the lifting connections to the panels of track, hanging loose. In other views they can be seen fixed to the rails by bolts mechanically slid under the rails and worked by the two levers sticking up on the bail head, which slide in the slots visible in the 'demonstration at Waterloo' photo (page 95). This photo shows how the bogie well vehicle has been adapted for its new purpose. Originally the lifting mechanisms were open to the elements, but sometime between 1948 and 1952 they were enclosed as shown by construction of the sheet metal sheds seen here.

Opposite lower - The second photo shows the lifting vehicle attached to the compressor vehicle with which it worked. The bales are shown in the stowed position, as are the arms, and these are secured by stay wires to the wagon frame to prevent movement in transit. A brief description of the vehicle seen here appeared in the book *British Railway Track, 2nd Edition,* first published in 1950, and some of the details contained therein are summarised here. The two lifting frames were spaced about 30 feet apart, which was considered a good distance to equalise sag between the lifting points on a 60 foot panel. The frames contained winches, which raised and lowered the panel lifting bales hanging from the jibs. The jibs, as can be seen in the photo, had a number of holes from which the bales hung. These were spaced 3" apart to suit varying six-foot distances. The TRM could therefore operate on tracks spaced anything from 4'6" to 7'0" apart. The jibs could also operate on either side of the vehicle, by turning on a central pivot. It was important that the TRM was balanced carefully when operating, to reduce the forces on the bogie springs on the side of the vehicle nearest the relaying. The article therefore refers to the wagon being equipped with extending counterbalance weights, which could be drawn out on the opposite side of the vehicle to the relaying operation. The required extension would take account of a number of factors including the weight lifted and the cant or

superelevation of the track. On completion, these counterbalance weights along with the jibs would all be stowed within the vehicle's normal loading gauge. These counter weights, are unfortunately, not clearly visible in these photos. Many of the early trials in Track Relaying Machine design used old rails strapped to the wagon floor to give the wagon more weight for stability. To facilitate loading of old panels of track onto the adjacent bogie wagons the jibs were fixed as high as practical within the standard loading gauge, ensuring that the machine could travel beneath normal bridges etc. Normal loading was five panels, but six could be handled if the track was bullhead, on lower bogie vehicles and on certain routes. As well as use on site, the vehicle would also be used in the Pre-Assembly Depots located around the system, where panels of track for relaying would be made up to a chart derived from exact measurements taken at the site. These charts would take into account the curvature of the track, the 'lead' of each rail (how much one rail extends in advance of the other), the positions of short sleepers around drains, the position of insulated joints and so forth, resulting in a set of panels built specifically for one site. The Southern used 59'7" rails on the inside of curves periodically to keep the joints within about 3" of square, which were derived by cutting one bolt hole off a standard rail and redrilling it. These short rails would be built in to new panels according to the site requirements at the PAD. Other railway companies surmounted the same problem in different ways - the GW, for example, used 59'9" rails specially cut and drilled. Panels would be built against a square end or allowance made for the lead or lag of the rails. Though all panels would be built nominally straight, and curved on site, this lead /lag of the low rail was important, or it would cause the sleepers to go very out-of-square once the track was actually laid at the relaying site, if it was set up incorrectly. As well as straining the fastenings, this would affect the track gauge. Occasionally, mistakes were made and panels built with the wrong hand. Some P Way workers can recount tales of track trying to curve the wrong way down the bank! The relaying machine would, of course, unload the old panels too after the relaying, back in the scrapping area of the depot. The relaying machines could deal with 60 foot panels of track of about 5 tons each (wood sleepered at this stage - concrete panels are much heavier). Occasionally some panels removed would be only 45', or even 30' long and short panels would be loaded on top of the wagons taking the old trackwork away from site, with longer panels below. Therefore sometimes there would be the need to sort panels on site. Fishplates for the joints would be fitted with bolts and loaded on the sleepers in the fourfoot, at the panel end in the PAD, so the plates were readily available on site. Panels were numbered. When considering the lifting ability of the machines, the 'drag' effect of the ballast had to be added to the weight of the panels when pulling the track out of the ballast. At that time renewal of the ballast was less common than it is now and the track was often opened out of ballast to the sleeper bottom to allow relaying and subsequently refilled with the old ballast before being topped up with some new stone. If you were unlucky enough to have to 'load' the dirty ballast by hand it was two men to a 10 ton open wagon as a turn of duty! Much more on the process of relaying and indeed maintenance of the track is contained in the above book, which has been regularly updated over the years, as the text book of all things relating to track. Older copies still appear at sales or are lovingly owned by older staff! Alternatively, it is available from The Permanent Way Institution.

Above and right - These show the diesel compressor, which provided compressed air by pipes and hoses to the lifting/sluing gear. It is also believed to have supplied the power to the lights (minimal by modern standards) seen on the jibs in the previous photos. As relaying took place at any time, the track could be given up to an engineering possession and therefore often took place overnight. This wagon is very basic! A large diesel engine powered the compressor and the compressed air was stored in the large round reservoir. The diesel fuel was stored in the central drums. Hand railing is provided, as the drums would need man-handling into position and priming etc. on site during the work. The wording on the diesel compressor side states 'Consolidated Pneumatics'

'STATE OF THE ART' TRACK RELAYING - 1948

Opposite lower - Taken in February 1948 at Hither Green, the wording on the rear of the photo states that this equipment is new. It is highly likely, therefore, that the smartly painted and, at this stage, uncovered equipment is being 'trialled in the yard'. An unidentified SECR 4-4-0 loco is being used to provide the propulsion for the TRM and its associated compressor wagon and the crew look on with interest! Self-propelled Track Relaying Machines were still some way off. As with many activities at this stage of development, some of the detail had yet to be worked out. Releasing the bales from the panel, for instance, meant you had to climb on top of the panel and manually release the bolts once the weight had been taken off them. You then had to climb down again for the next panel to be loaded, and back up to release that one and so on. In the dark, on slippery sleepers without any handrails etc., this could be a dangerous job. Equally, walking along the panel in the wet when stacked, meant you had to be very careful not to slip between sleepers. The panels were often loaded 5 high, sometimes 6, and in the depots higher still when stacked on the ground. It's no mean feet to climb up dirty slippery track to the top of a pile that high - on a wagon, your head was nearly 16 feet from the unforgiving ground! The track panels were, of course, chained down in transit. The sleepers therefore could be 9 foot long if old, which is close to the standard loading gauge – and even if they were newer and only 8'6" long nominally, the rails weren't always quite central, particularly if sleepers had been changed or re-bored on site. Therefore extreme care was therefore taken in loading the sleepers to avoid them sticking out. Any that did so might have to be cut off or removed in some cases. Generally, however, the panels would fit reasonably easily within the loading gauge, provided care was taken when loading. On completion and before the train was despatched 'The Examiner' would check, reloading was not popular…

A demonstration to the General Public at Waterloo Platform 5 on the 19th July 1948. This picture actually pre-dates the others. Taken just after the end of the war, it may have been taken to show how the railways intended to try and move forward from their huge backlog of relaying at the time. The caption refers to the fact that the relaying was actually taking place between the morning and evening rush hours. 840ft, in 60ft panels, was being relaid with about 40 men assisting. The work obviously attracted a good crowd, who, generously, were admitted free to stand and watch the proceedings! The work didn't commence, apparently, until 11.00 and used the most up to date TRM available (without covers to the winches or jibs at each end yet). The actual relaying of the track was apparently completed in four hours. It doesn't say what work then took place, but presumably the 'con rail' was also replaced and at least some ballast restored in the time, although the amount of lifting and packing completed before the evening rush hour was probably minimal. Note again that the ballast has not been dug, merely opened to the sleeper base to give a nominally level surface for the new track. This picture shows an old 45' panel coming out. The con rail, which swaps sides at the platform end, to keep it away from the public side, is seen displaced under the panel. Guard boarding has been laid aside along with some of the ballast. The old track would be loaded onto one lot of bogie wagons and the new track provided on others. As wagons became empty they could be reloaded and for many years they were moved over bridging pieces (or just a small gap) from the new to the old track, to allow further use on the other part of the relaying train, which had been provided at the site for the work. Of course, loading and unloading of wagons had to be done logically, as the TRM couldn't lift a panel over a fully loaded bogie wagon. On the top of the panel lifting bales, the release levers for the lifting bolts can be seen working in the slots. The bolt can just be seen below the leading left hand rail. The relaying machine is the same type as that seen above, but the compressor is in one four-wheel wagon and the air reservoir in another. The whole arrangement has still to be situated on one bogie wagon. It can clearly be seen that the jib accommodates various positions at 3" centres for allowance for different six foots, although some juggling on site would still be required as track doesn't always follow neat sixfoots in three inch increments! Use of the size 10 boot can be seen in this photo…

There is a feeling of anticipation in this photo, with people poised for the next move, though this had probably been well rehearsed beforehand in a yard. It may, of course, be just the interest in new and badly needed technology. The crowd seem very interested, presumably taking their lunch break to watch. A portion of the left hand track to Platform 6 appears to have already been relaid. One last job after loading all the panels on bogie wagons for removal from site was to remove loose stones off sleepers - if they came off a panel train passing through a station they could become serious missiles!

COLOUR INTERLUDE

For this issue our colour section comes from the camera of Roger Thornton / Kevin Robertson collection.
As is often the way a chance remark and conversation led to a fascinating afternoon viewing some of his remarkable colour collection. The results can be seen over the next few pager.

Above - 30587 is depicted on a loaded clay train at Boscarne Junction 22nd July 1960.

THE 8.15 am GETS A WASH AND BRUSH UP

Left - A couple of issues ago we asked for material reference the electric carriage sheds that were constructed in several parts of the system mainly from the 1920s onwards. Well, not exactly the same, but close enough and thanks to Steven James for submitting the photograph. The location is Orpington on 27th March 1946, and with the delightful caption on the reverse of the print that is shown. The unit is a 2-NOL.